T0303838

NOW THAT'S WHAT I CALL JARROW

Paul Perry

AMBERLEY

First published 2022

Amberley Publishing
The Hill, Stroud, Gloucestershire, GL5 4EP
www.amberley-books.com

ISBN 978 1 3981 0217 0 (print)
ISBN 978 1 3981 0218 7 (ebook)

British Library Cataloguing in Publication Data.
A catalogue record for this book is available from the British Library.

Typesetting by SJmagic DESIGN SERVICES, India.
Printed in Great Britain.

CONTENTS

Introduction	4
Around the Town	6
Best Days of Your Life	20
Regeneration and Housing	40
Time Gentlemen, Please	63
Highways and Byways	76
Acknowledgements	96

INTRODUCTION

Jarrow has witnessed many changes since its humble beginnings in the fifth century, when it was referred to as Gyrwy, an Anglo-Saxon name, which roughly translated means 'marsh dwellers'. These changes, very often major, and others not quite so significant, have gone largely unnoticed. It is most difficult to publish any written work about Jarrow without giving reference to the Venerable Bede, the Jarrow Crusade and the mighty Palmers' empire, which had been the throbbing heart of the town for decades. But on this occasion, and for the nature of this publication, it is within their relative positions in the town's often complex history they must remain, at least in the interim.

During the 1960s, the priority for the majority of the younger generation was securing a job and eventually raising a family. For working-class people there was no better place to be than Jarrow, with a wealth of industry and factories on their doorstep after the town emerged like a phoenix from the ashes of doom and gloom, reminiscent of the depression of the thirties. Jarrow was once again a thriving town with so much to offer. It is highly probable that the construction of the Arndale Centre was a contributing factor in the turnaround of the town's recently found prosperity. The centre boasted an excess of 100 shops, and parking spaces for more than 200 vehicles, not to mention leisure facilities.

Towards the end of the decade, Jarrow was in a sound financial position thanks to a period of economic growth, and it became one of the most modern go-ahead towns on Tyneside. Many aspects of the town were recognised nationally as a showpiece of inner-city civic development. This was largely due to the demolition of most of the ageing back-to-back terraces of accommodation and several corner shops. The corner shops which did survive battled for a slice of the market, diversifying with promotions, special offers and a larger range of goods as a means of survival, in an attempt to compete with the brightly lit supermarkets, such as Moore's in Bede Precinct and Presto in Viking Precinct, which made a dramatic entrance and impact on the way the residents shopped, offering the convenience of pre-packed comestibles and a huge range of fast foods direct from a chilled cabinet. The domestic kitchen became more user-friendly with the use of appliances and gadgets from retailers Thomas & Richley in Ellison Street, and the Co-op located in Centenary House offered an impressive and competitive range of white goods and kitchen equipment.

By 1971, the nation was waking up to decimalisation, and restrictions on power usage were to become normal, at least for a while as the miners worked to rule. By 1973, the country's coal reserves had become dangerously low, forcing the government to act as the power grid struggled to meet demand, initially by rationing electricity for non-essential services to three days a week. This was followed by interruptions to domestic supplies, resulting in the population adjusting their lives accordingly as their homes and streets were plunged into darkness.

Through the days of triumph and tragedy, the outstanding feature of Jarrow has been its people. Famous writers, singers, local characters and villains have all grown up in the town, but it is the ordinary Jarovian possessing a rare mixture of honesty and decency that has contributed to the town's unique personality. In return, all are marked forever by the town and have a genuine affection for it. So, let us have one more glimpse down the years into the schoolyards and churches, the factories and the shops. Let us meet the men and women, our mothers and fathers perhaps, or even ourselves in younger days. You don't need your hat or your coat, you don't even have to leave the comfort of your armchair – just turn the page and travel once more along the streets and back lanes of your town, my town, our town: Jarrow.

Paul Perry
2020

AROUND THE TOWN

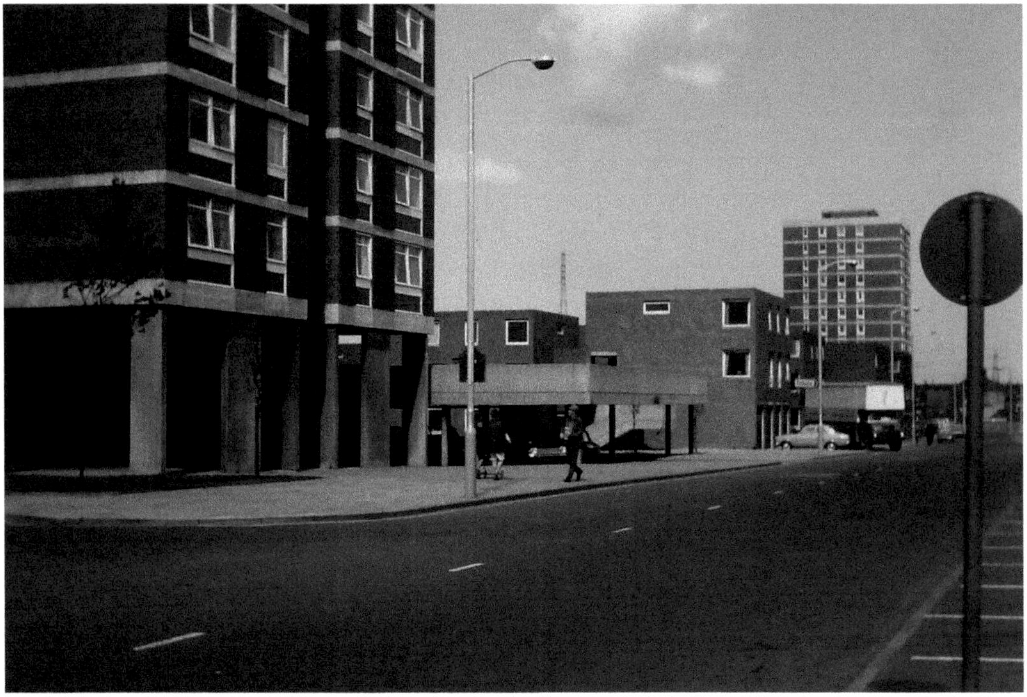

Central Area

Formerly a thriving and vibrant shopping thoroughfare and bus route, Grange Road today is little more than a quiet walkway to the shopping precincts of the Viking Centre, providing sufficient parking in this now-residential area of the town. The original council housing estate featured in this 1972 photograph was demolished during the 1990s and replaced with smart and sought-after private accommodation.

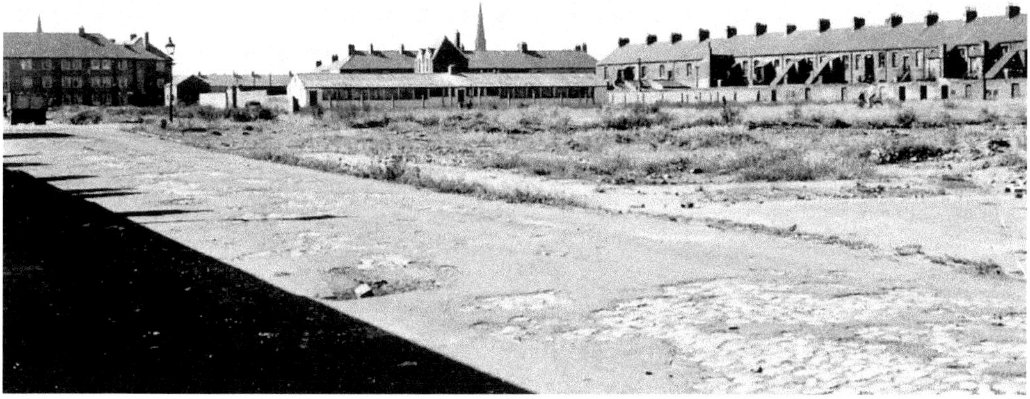

Dunn Street School

After a devastating bombing raid on Jarrow in 1941, Dunn Street School was damaged beyond repair. Surprisingly, the schoolhouse visible in the centre of this image from 1960 suffered minimal damage. The school's main building was temporarily replaced with a prefabricated building for the continuation of school procedures, until the site was demolished around 1965.

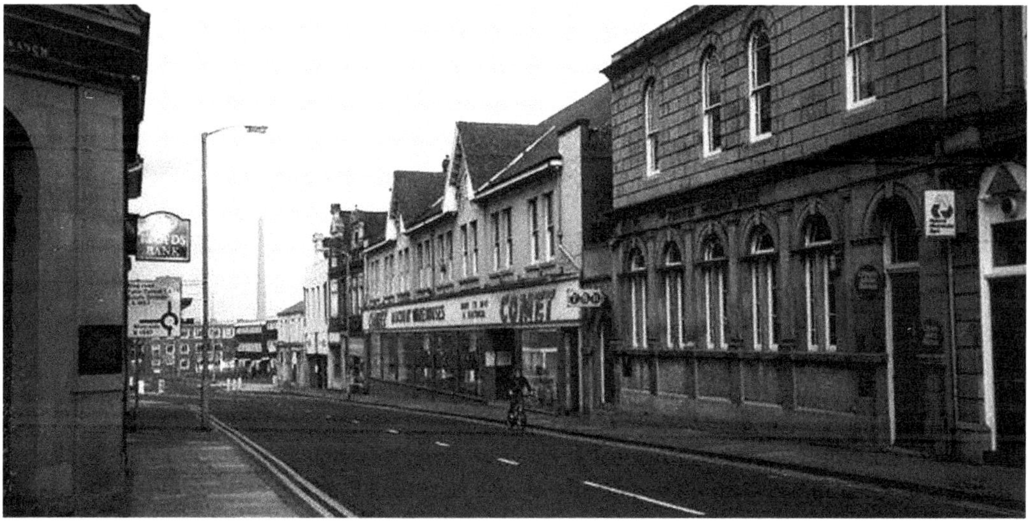

Ellison Street

This part of Ellison Street was primarily the gateway to the industrial part of the town, which hugged the south bank of the illustrious River Tyne. The building to the right of the photograph occupied by Comet was originally the Royal Albert Hall, until it was devastated by fire in 1913. After extensive refurbishment, the structure of the building remained largely the same, with the exception of the facia, which was totally transformed. During the 1920s and 1930s, the upper floors were utilised as a billiard hall, and later the entire building became a department store, Shephards of Gateshead. This photograph dates from 1981.

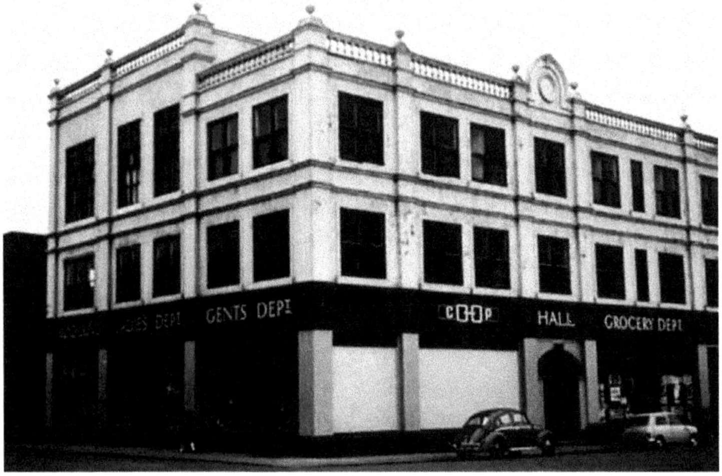

North Street

The Jarrow Industrial Co-operative Society was formed in 1861 from premises in Commercial Road, and from 1892, the name changed to the more familiar Jarrow & Hebburn Co-operative Society. The Market Square was largely given over to the society from which to trade. The prominent, white stucco-faced buildings were a feature of the town for many years, comprising of a department store, which became the Cavalier Club during the 1970s. The accompanying photograph of the Store Hall – as it was commonly known just prior to its demolition in the 1980s – formed community rooms and a dance venue.

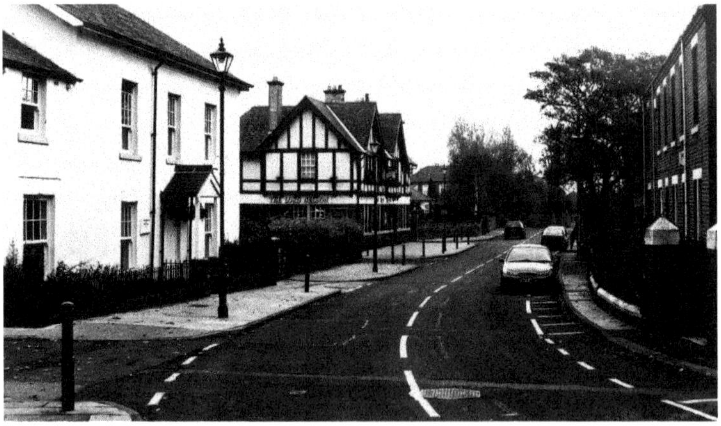

Monkton Village

It was to Monkton Village that Benedictine monks fled after the desolation of their seventh-century monastery on the banks of the River Don during the eleventh century. Originally, the village situated between Jarrow & Hebburn was totally independent of both towns and even had its own governing body: Jarrow Council presided over the affairs of the village from around 1932. Today, the picturesque little village forms part of the metropolitan borough of South Tyneside. This images dates from 1987.

Grange Road

High-rise living came to Jarrow during the 1960s, with three multistorey blocks of flats: Wilkinson, Ellen and Monastery courts. These luxury concierge-controlled apartments were flanked either side by the self-contained maisonettes of the Grange and North courts. However, as the 1980s dawned, the council owned properties were showing severe signs of neglect and consequently demolished. This resulted in the construction of private accommodation being built on the former Market Square development site. After a sensitive refurbishing programme by STMBC, the tower blocks survived. This image dates from around 1980.

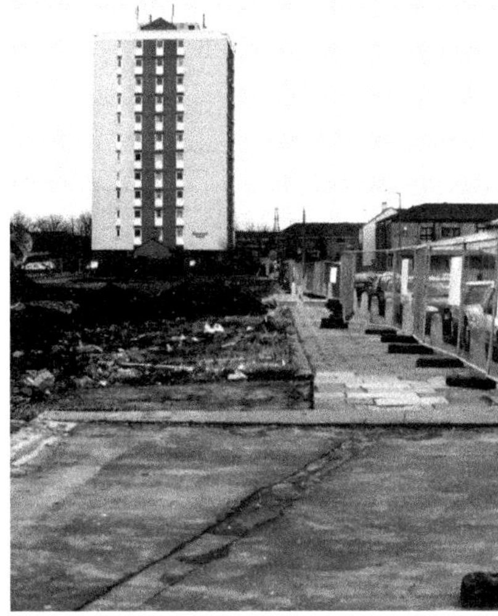

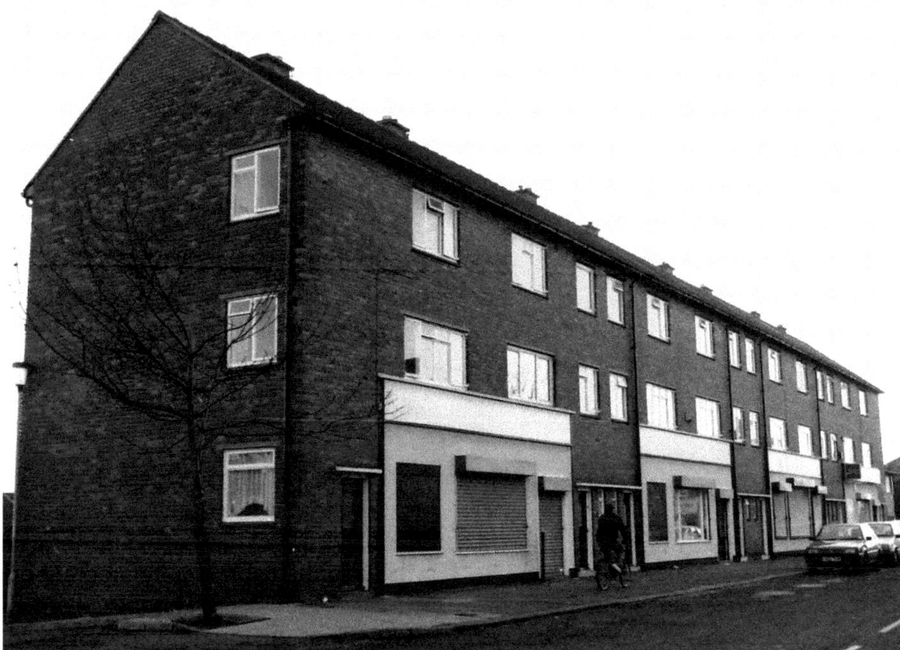

High Street

When these maisonettes were constructed in High Street in 1952, they were highly sought after, classed amongst the most desirable residences in the town centre at that time. The conveniently positioned retail outlets were considered to be an added bonus for residents lucky enough to be granted a tenancy for the council-owned property. The shops, which became available the same year, were occupied by a newsagent, family butcher, greengrocer and grocery store, catering for most of the resident's daily requirements. This image dates from 1989.

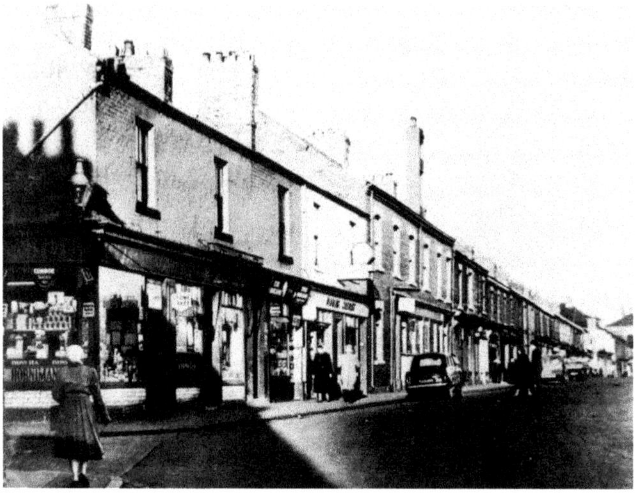

Monkton Road

Prior to the popularity of television during the 1960s, radio seemed to be the nation's sole source of verbal communication. Families often huddled around a tiny Bakelite radio – which had been turned on and tuned in five minutes in advance to allow an assortment of valves and other components to 'warm up' – and listen in silence to the evening's entertainment. Other devices popular at this time were powered by an accumulator – an early form of battery, which, when run down, had to be recharged at Winchesters in Monkton Road.

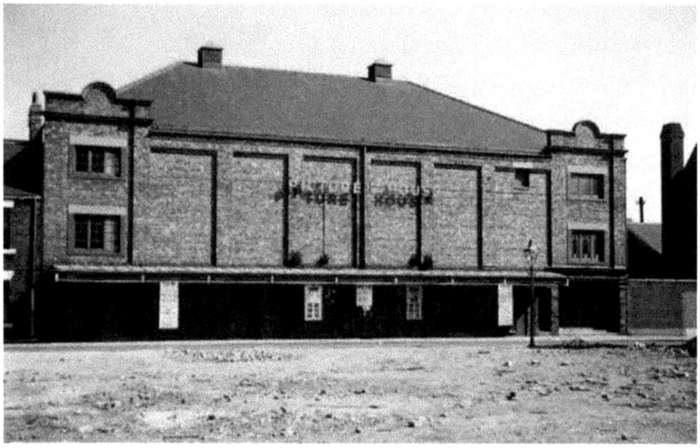

Picture House

During the 1950s and 1960s, it was the cinema which reigned supreme as most people's chosen night out. For one and a tanner (7.5p) cinema goers could expect the evening's main event: a 'B' movie and a selection of glossy advertisements from media advertising giants Pearl & Dean. The decline of the cinema came about as television gained popularity. Jarrow's three cinemas, Regal, Picture House and Empire, all witnessed dwindling audiences within a short space of time, but found another lease of life as bingo halls, at least for a short while until the craze declined. Pictured: the Picture House in North Street 1973.

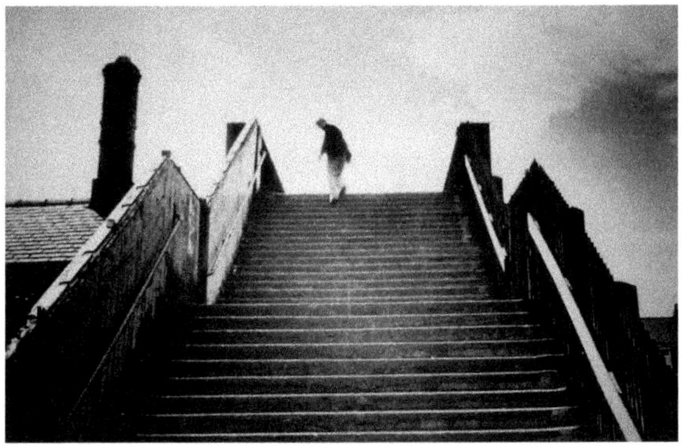

Station Stairs

The station stairs, as the structure became known, was erected in 1884, connecting two points of the town centre either side of the mineral line, and had recently introduced passenger railway lines. By 1891, the open-topped popular and necessary crossing was under revision to include a safe crossing for horse- and hand-drawn carts. However, plans were abandoned due to disagreements over financial backing by both parties: the railway authorities and the town council. Eventually, a compromise was reached, and the structure was reinforced enough to support the weight of a glass canopy. It remained this way until its demolition in the 1970s, and it was replaced with the Metro crossing during the 1980s. Pictured: demolition of the station stairs during the 1970s.

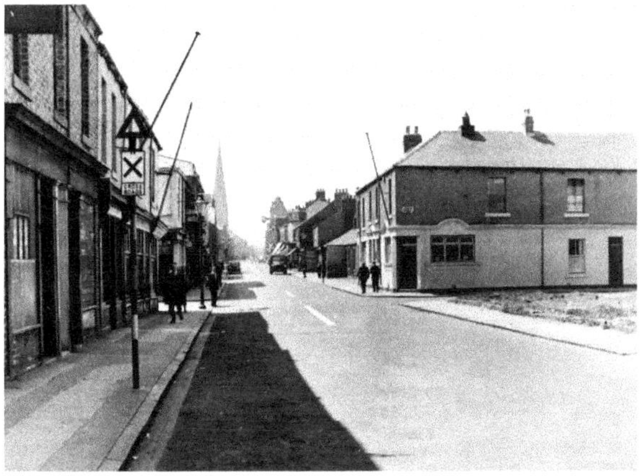

Working Men's Clubs

Working men's clubs were popularised in 1862, at the founding of the institute by clergyman Rev Henry Solly. The members-only institutions were affiliated to the Club & Institute Union (CIU), a governing body ensuring the establishments were operated to strict rules and regulations. The principal purpose of the organisation was to provide a voice at national level and to offer discounted goods and services for members and bona fide guests. The Royal British Legion, the Royal Association of the Order of Buffaloes, and the Ex-Servicemen's Club were prolific in Jarrow for many years. The original Ex-Servicemen's Club in Grange Road is on the right of the accompanying photograph.

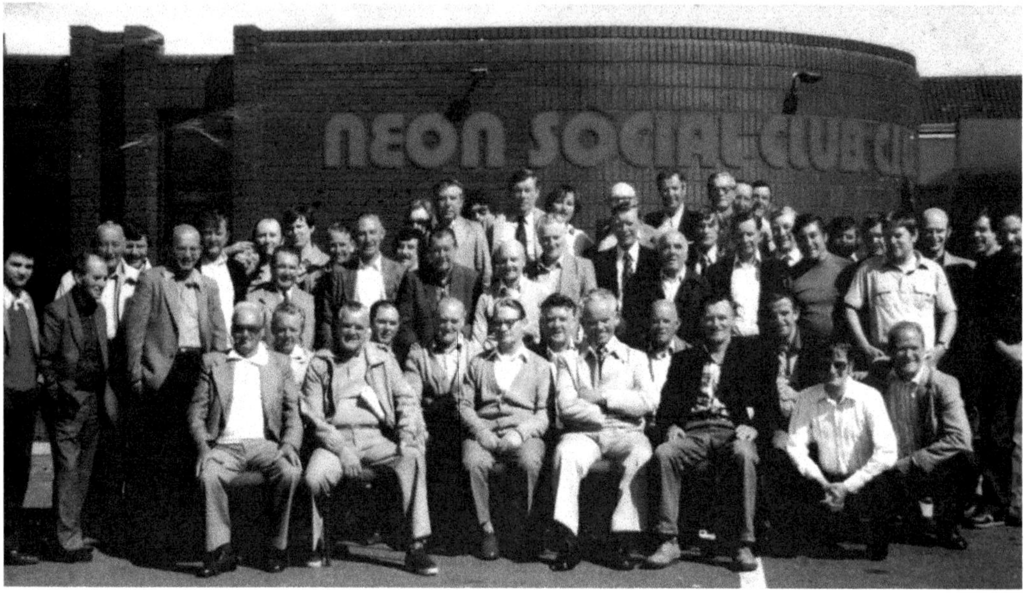

Neon Social Club

Above and below: The only two surviving clubs in the town centre are the former R.A.O.B, now renamed the Ellison Social Club, in Ellison Street, and The Alberta Club in Grant Street. The popular Gasworks Club in Grange Road in the 1950s was renamed the Neon Social Club when it was relocated to Nairn Street on the South Leam Estate during the 1960s. Alas, due to falling membership numbers and viability, the building was demolished in 2019. Pictured: The Neon Social Club during demolition and the members' annual outing to the races during the 1970s.

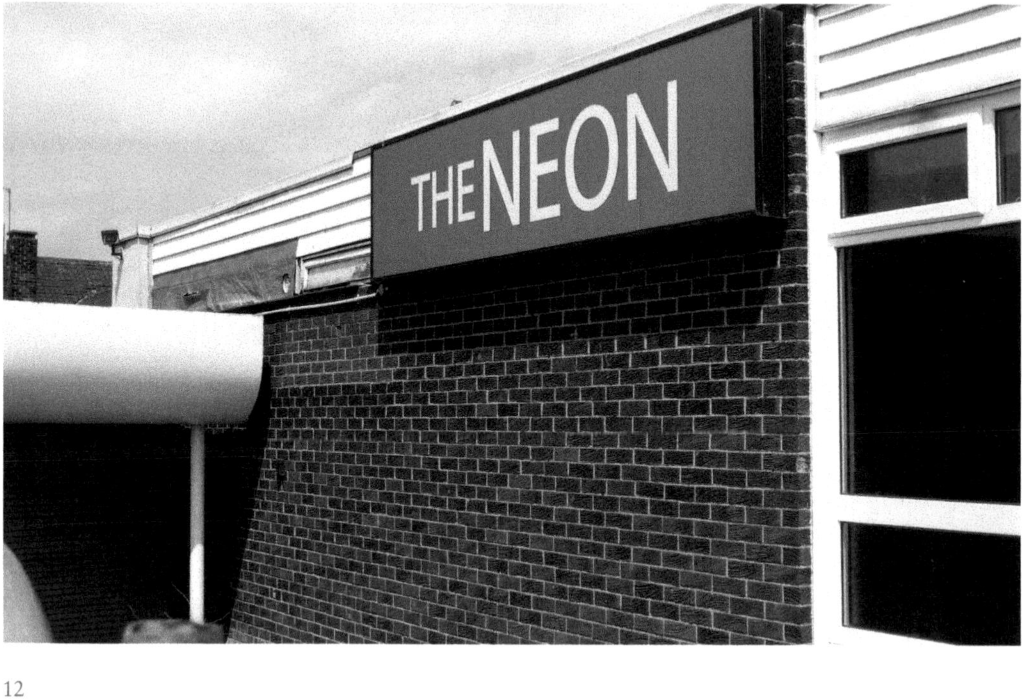

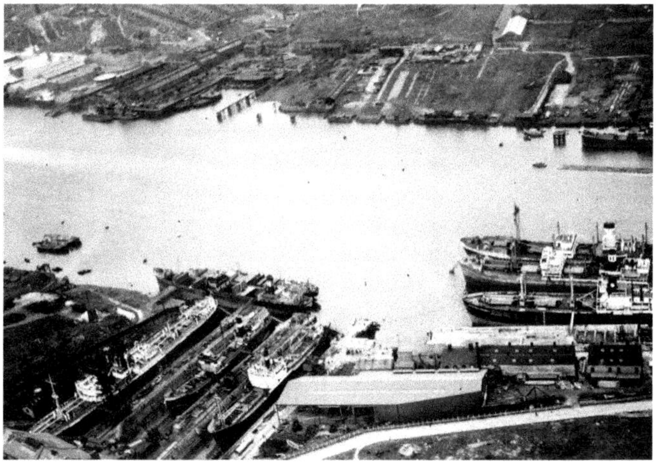

Mercantile Engineering Company

The Mercantile Engineering Co. commenced trading in Jarrow in 1885 and flourished in the town for close to a century. The successful ship repair company provided work for thousands of men residing either side of the river. From the 1960s, the yard changed ownership several times, and as ships became more reliable, fewer passed this way, creating a rapid decline in the ship-repairing industry. This striking image of the area clearly shows the concentration of industry in this area of the town.

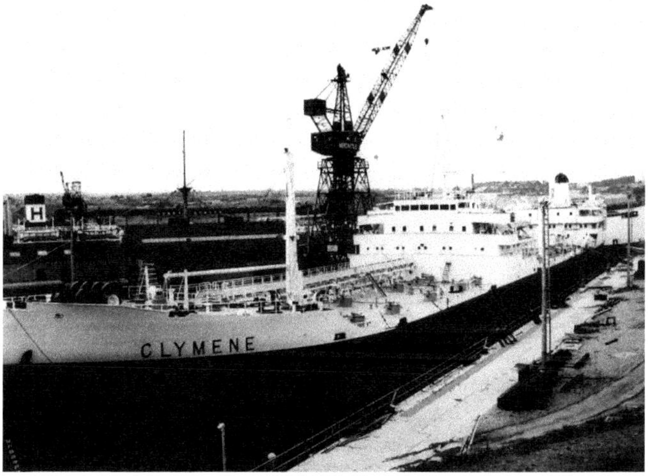

Mercantile Dry Dock

A new addition to the Jarrow skyline was visible from 1948: an impressive monster crane was erected at the Mercantile Dry Dock & Engineering Co. in Curlew Road. The installation of the mono-tower crane, rising 180 feet above the riverbank, was a major contribution to the yard's facilities and extensive modernisation programme. This crane could lift an impressive 15 tonnes at a radius of 90 feet and 6 tonnes at a radius of 126 feet. It was designed to travel on rails, similar to that of a train, and serve three dry docks.

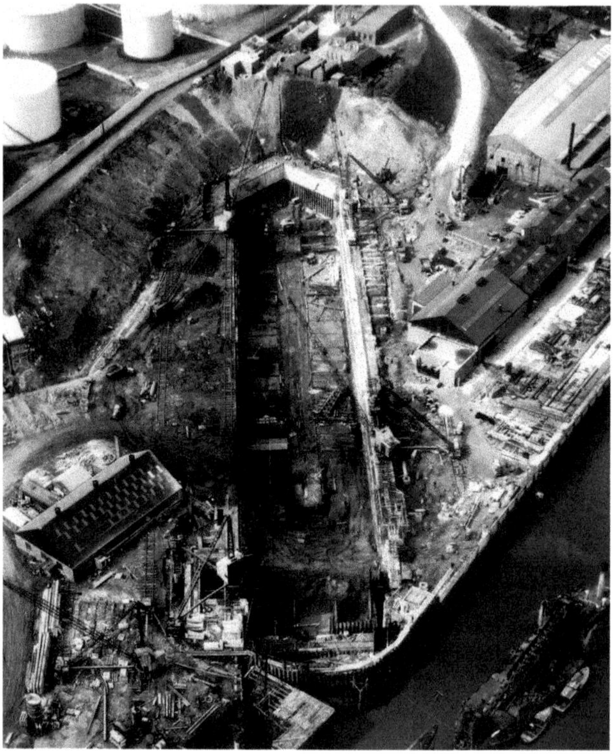

Mercantile Dry Dock

The company's 1960s restructuring regime saw a fairly stable and promising period, with a sustained stream of colliers, tankers and cargo boats drawing up for refit and repair. The gigantic No. 4 dry dock was completed in 1960 to accommodate the larger vessels that were now beginning to make up the world fleet, so the company looked towards a brighter and more prosperous future. Pictured: The impressive No. 4 dry dock nearing completion in 1961.

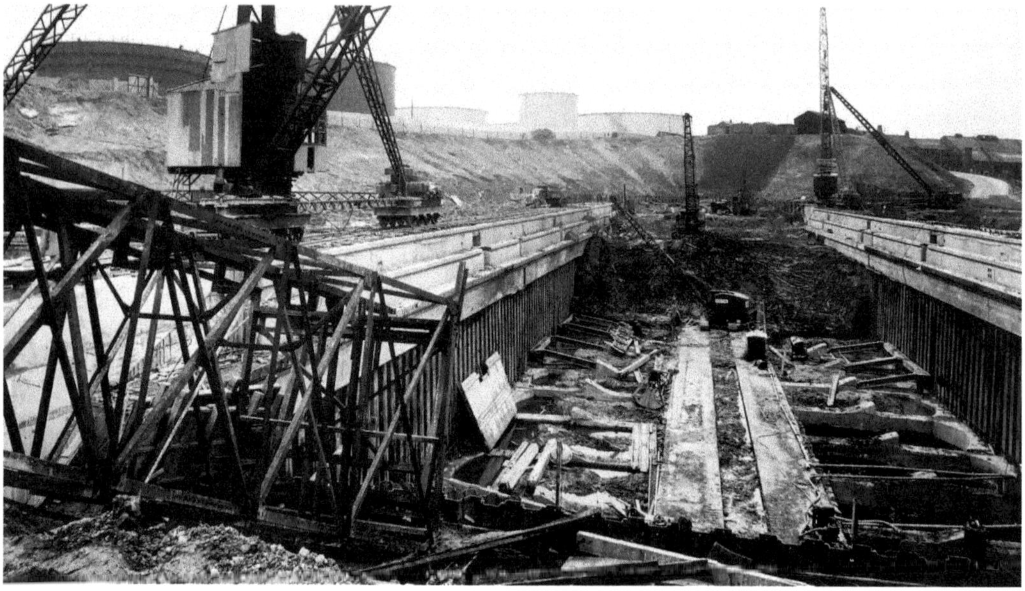

Mercantile Dry Dock

By 1966, the company became a subsidiary of North East Coast Ship Repairers Ltd, then a constituent company of the Court Line Shipping Group of Companies. The Tyne Ship Repair Group were to take over the day-to-day running of the yard's operations until its demise in 1981.

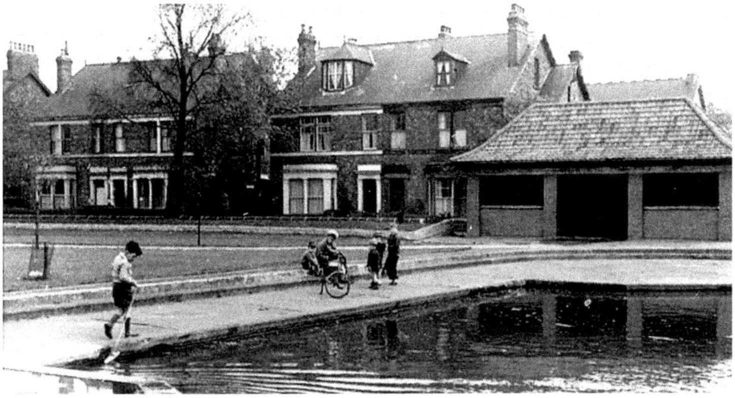

Parkland

During the 1960s, Jarrow council was one of the only boroughs in the land that was totally void of rent arrears. This meant the financial position was cash positive and in a better place than in previous years, and with cash to spend the council wasted no time refurbishing the town's parkland, which had been sadly neglected. Council gardeners maintained the town's five parks to a very high standard. Currently, the parks and cemetery are expertly tended by a team of volunteers who work tirelessly producing colourful flower bed displays throughout the summer months. Pictured here is West Park in 1960.

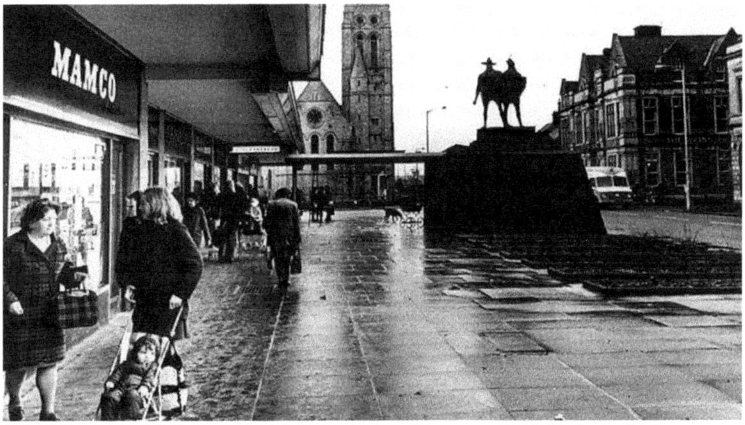

Grange Road

Men's and women's fashion had suddenly taken a step in the right direction during the 1960s, with the development and accessibility of a huge range of fabrics from around the world that manufacturers were keen to purchase. But perhaps the most welcome change in fashion was for young men, who found an innermost pride and no longer dressed conservatively, relishing the brightly coloured shirts with huge collars, hipster trousers and the obligatory Cuban heeled shoes. This less formal style of dress came at a price, courtesy of Marcus Price Boutique in Newcastle, to those who could afford to shop there; for the less fortunate, Chris B. Watson in Grange Road and Masons outfitters in Arndale Arcade were a satisfactory and affordable alternative. This photograph of Grange Road dates from 1969.

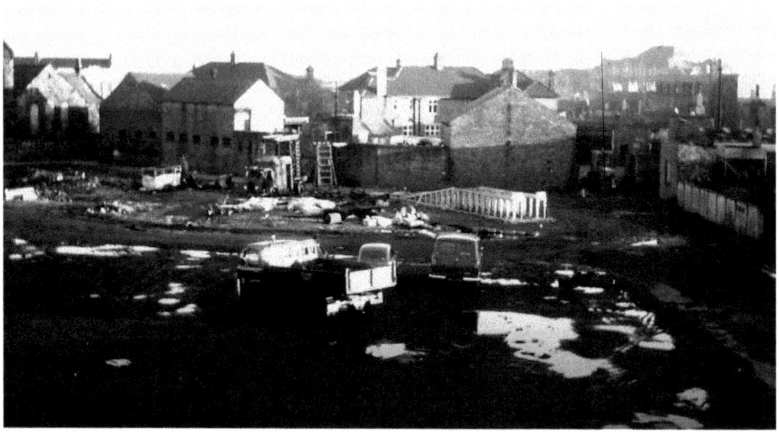

Former Council Building Depot

Just as the new decade was dawning in 1960, Jarrow still had quite a lot of work to do demolishing houses deemed unfit for human habitation. As the local economy was vibrant and the rising consumer trend towards spending looked set to continue, there were many opportunities for employment in all areas of the town, which included commerce and of course what the town was famous for: ship repair. Jarrow Corporation was employing apprentices by the score across all sectors of their building programme; this created the promise of a brighter future as security and prosperity were just visible on the horizon. Pictured: Former council building depot in Ellison Street being dismantled in 1975.

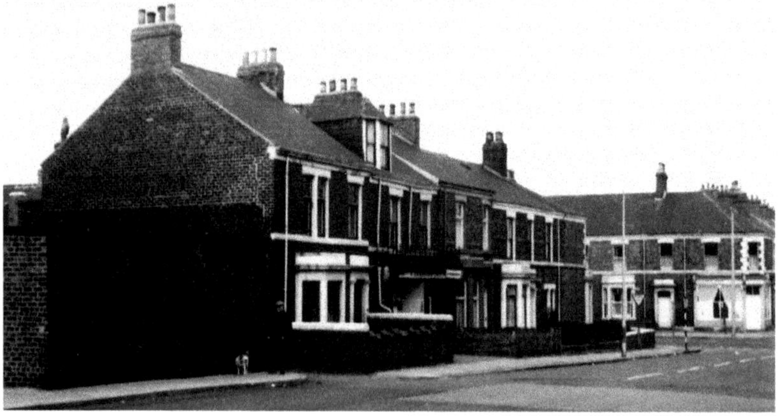

Park Road

Rising volumes of traffic during the late 1960s were proving to be a problem for Jarrow. Transport executives introduced measures to relieve the streets of the unwelcome burden of noise and pollution, which was becoming an increasing nuisance. One-way traffic-calming measures were placed at strategic points in the town, including Surrey Street and Kent Street, together with the relocation of traffic signals from the junction of Albert Road and Bede Burn Road to their present position at the foot of Park Road. A ring road around the perimeter of the town became an asset in the rerouting of heavy traffic from the town centre.

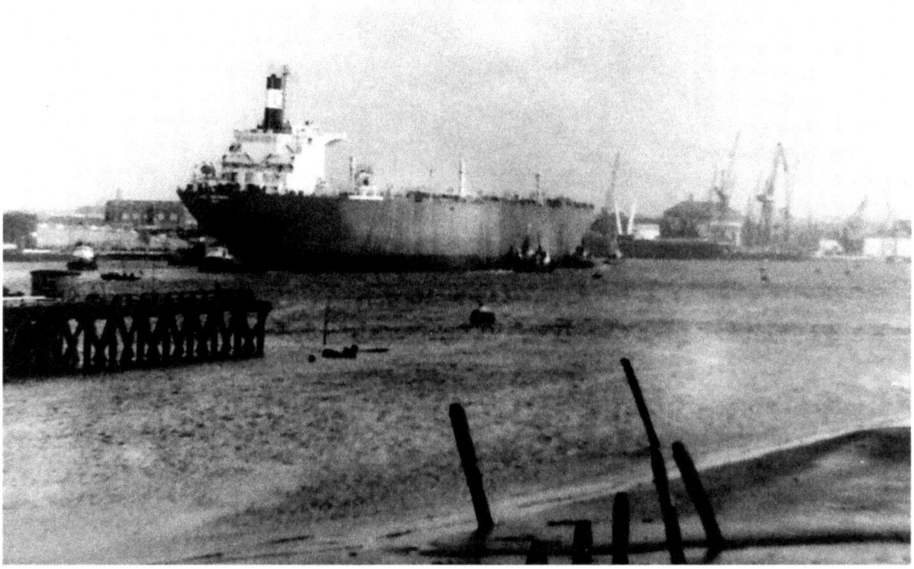

Esso Northumbria

In May 1969, the environment hit the headlines in a spectacular fashion when the first in a series of super tankers, *Esso Northumbria*, was launched at the Swan Hunter shipyard at Wallsend. It was a momentous occasion for the whole of Tyneside, and Princess Anne performed the launch ceremony of the largest vessel ever to be built in Britain. The 152,000-tonne crude oil carrier slipped gently and effortlessly into the murky waters of the River Tyne, a river which thousands of men relied upon for their livelihoods. Pictured: The monster *Esso Northumbria* at Jarrow preparing for sea trials in the North Sea in 1970.

Jarvis Park

The simple street games children played during the 1950s continued to be part of the street scene well into the 1960s. During the long, hot summer months, children amused themselves from sunrise to sunset with anything they could lay their hands on. A length of discarded washing line made an ideal skipping rope, while two pullovers doubled as goalposts. Hopscotch and hide-and-seek are memories from a distant past. Pictured: Children playing at Jarvis Park.

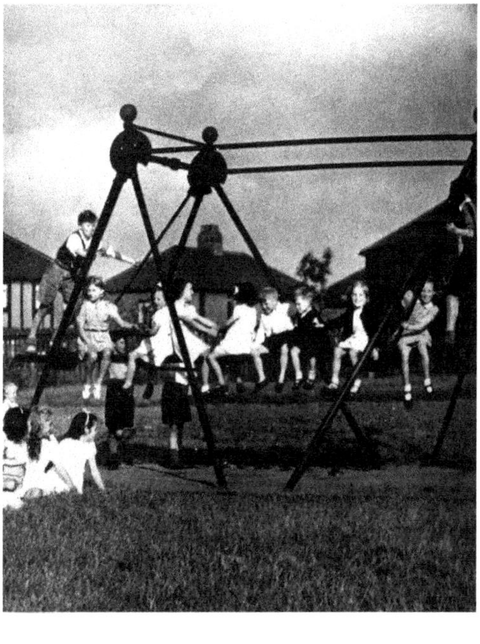

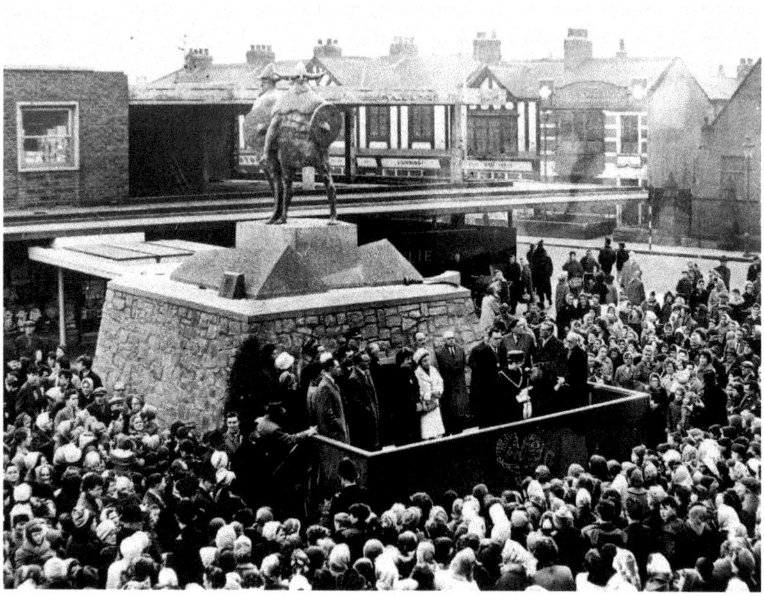

Viking Warriors

Above and below: The erection of commemorative sculptures in Jarrow commenced in 1877 with a drinking fountain presented to the town by confectioner Alderman Thomas Sheldon, which was sited close to the entrance of West Park. The Longmore Memorial Fountain was erected at the junction of Ellison Street and Grange Road in 1891, in memory of Joseph Longmore, founding member of the Venerable Bede Lodge & Sons of Temperance in Jarrow. It was relocated to Springwell Park around 1921. The Charles Palmer statue by sculptor Albert Toft in was unveiled in 1904. In 1921, the management behind Palmer donated the cenotaph in Clayton Street in memory of those who lost their lives in the First World War. Much later, in 1962, and to mark the opening of the Arndale Centre, a sculpture of two Viking warriors was unveiled in Grange Road. The arrival of the sculpture was received with mixed feelings from Jarrow folk as it commemorated two bloody invasions in AD 795 and again in AD 866, during which they decimated the Anglo-Saxon monastery. Pictured: The opening ceremony in 1962, and my brother, ten-year-old Malcolm, patiently awaiting their construction.

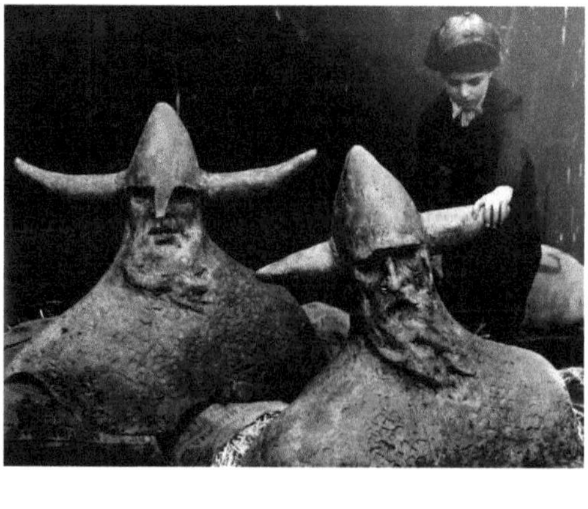

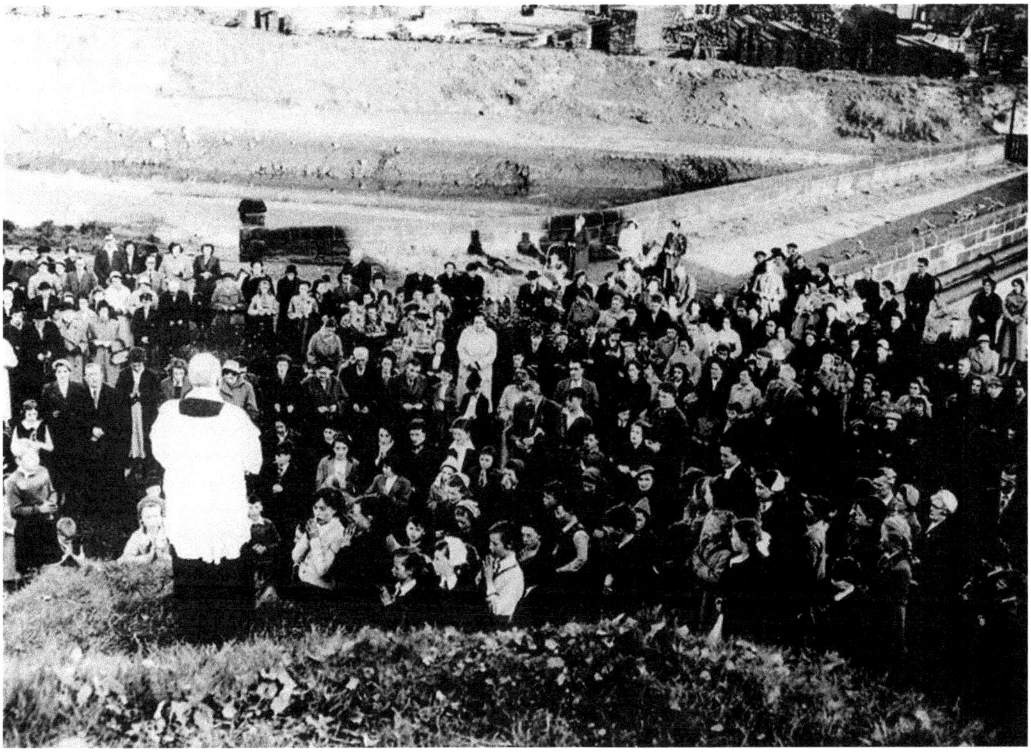

Canon Wilfrid Blenkin

Above and right: The feast day of the town's patron saint, Bede, is 26 May, which was for several years a memorable local celebration in the religious calendar. A procession from St Bede's Church in the town centre to the ruins of the ancient monastery in east Jarrow culminated in a thanksgiving service on the banks of the River Don. The service of remembrance was for several years conducted by parish priest Father Wilfrid Blenkin. Facilities were always made available for the occasion at St Paul's Church, but it is believed the stubborn cleric refused to conduct a Roman Catholic service in a Church of England premises. The traditional annual gathering ceased to exist from 1972, after the death of the canonised Wilfrid Blenkin. Pictured: The gathering on the banks of the Tyne, and hundreds of parishioners lining the streets to witness his funeral procession.

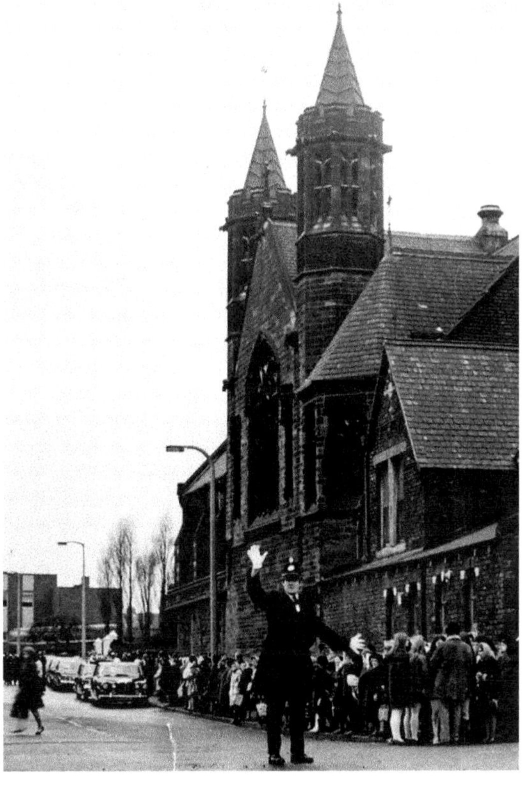

BEST DAYS OF YOUR LIFE

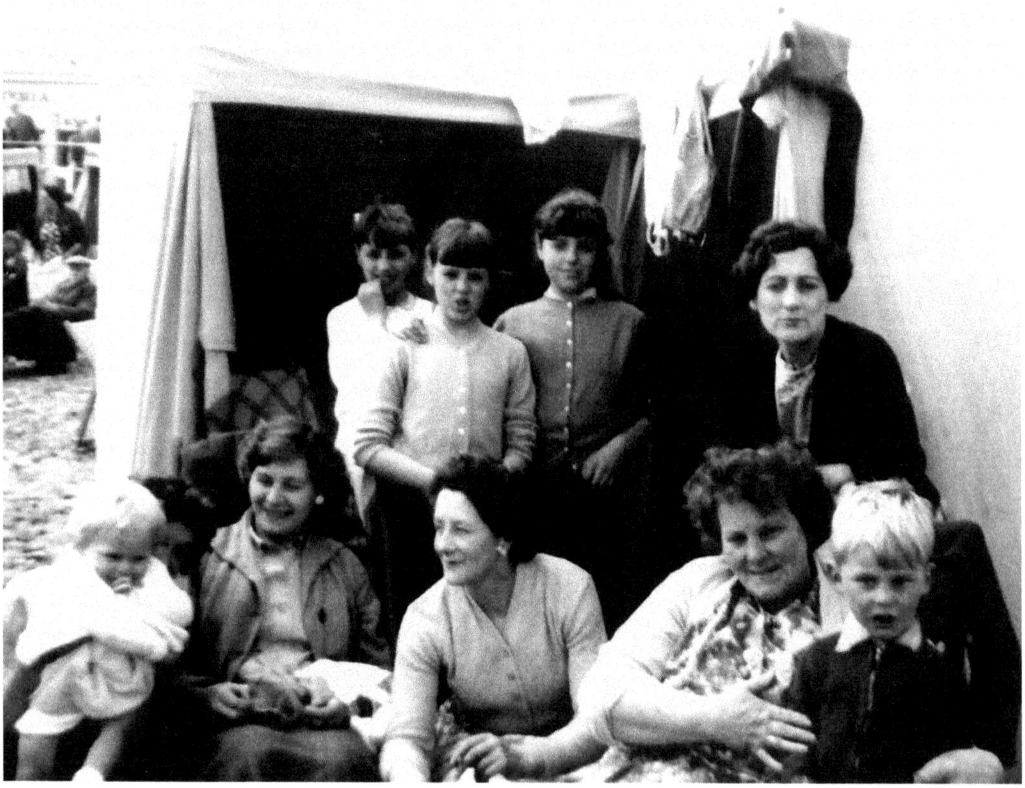

Summer Sun

Summertime entertainment for Jarrow folk during the 1960s centred around the beaches at South Shields and Whitley Bay. Clean sands free from pollution made these ideal playgrounds during the long, hot summer months for children of all ages. British seaside holiday resorts flourished during the 1960s, as sunseekers packed the beaches in every major resort. During the latter years of the decade, the package holidays to far off places were proving popular among those with a disposable income. Pictured: Jarrow folk enjoying the summer sun at South Shields.

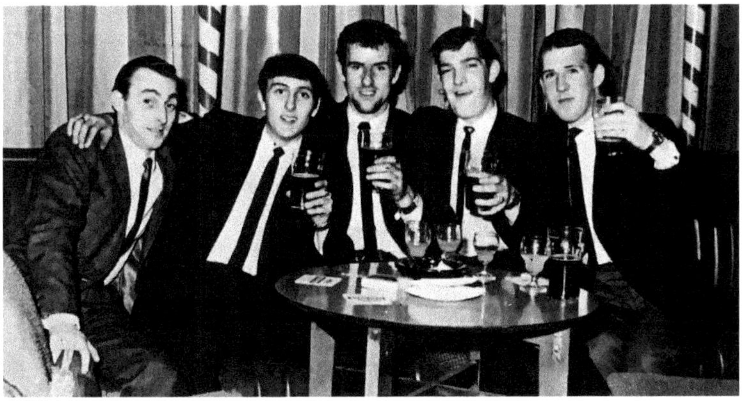

Nightlife

Above and below: During the 'Swinging 60s' Jarrow had been liberated. This liberation had been a long time coming, but people now had a disposable income to spend in any way they chose. Fashions were changing rapidly, and boutiques were springing up in every town, cashing in on the teenagers' new-found wealth. By 1965, the 'Flower Power' era had arrived from America, a non-violence ideology strongly opposed to the atrocities of the Vietnam War. This 'hippie' movement, as it was known, attracted flamboyantly dressed individuals who listened to psychedelic music while wearing floral embroidered clothing and flowers in their hair, both attributed to a sign of peace. This new wave of young men and women in their modern and fashionable attire turned heads as they fought the fashion war of the casual versus elegant on the dance floors of the many night spots that were now appearing on the High Street. For north-east England, the Baily Organisation bucked the trend with the Latino in South Shields, and followed this with similar venues in Newcastle, Sunderland and Middlesbrough. For Jarrow folk, Club Franchi, an Italian themed nightspot, was the place to be and be noticed. Pictured: Smartly dressed young men at Club Franchi in 1967.

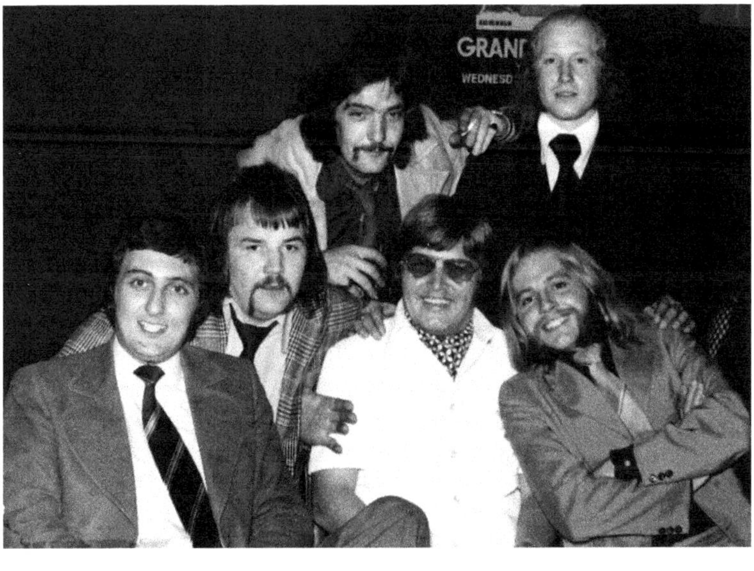

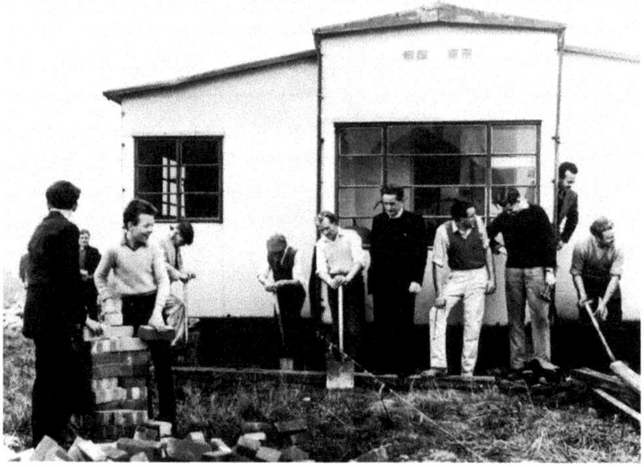

St Joseph's Parish

Above and below: In 1962, Father Christopher Rice came to Jarrow with the intention of forming a parish on the recently completed Hedworth Estate. After its formation there remained the small problem of where to celebrate mass, as the parish was without a church. The only available building in the area deemed large enough was the Boldon Lad public house, and Father Rice sought permission from the bishop, who authorised the proposal. The inaugural mass of the recently formed parish of St Joseph the Worker was celebrated on 13 May 1962 for 192 parishioners, who raised £100 for the purchase of a disused prefabricated building that was used as a temporary church for 10 years until sufficient funds were raised and the present church was built in 1972. St Joseph's School opened on 3 September 1968, with just sixty-five pupils, two teachers and Miss Margaret McArdle as head teacher. After a steady influx of pupils in the ensuing years, the school celebrated its fiftieth anniversary in 2018. Today, the school, with spaces for over 200 pupils, is managed by a dedicated team in a relaxed and pleasant atmosphere and is a thriving community with strong links between school and parish. Pictured: Father Christopher Rice and parishioners during construction of the temporary church in 1962, and St Joseph's Parish Council from 1972.

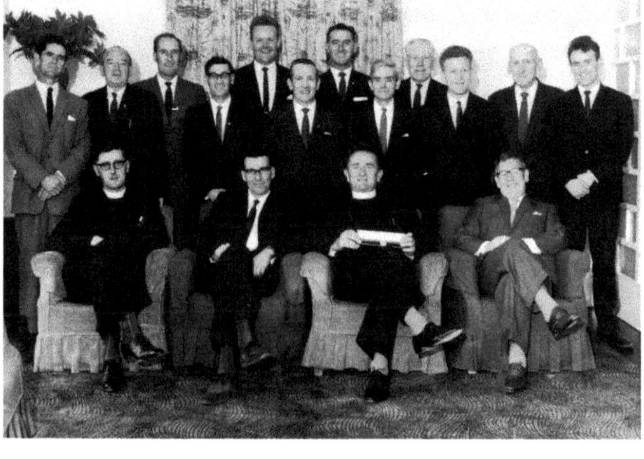

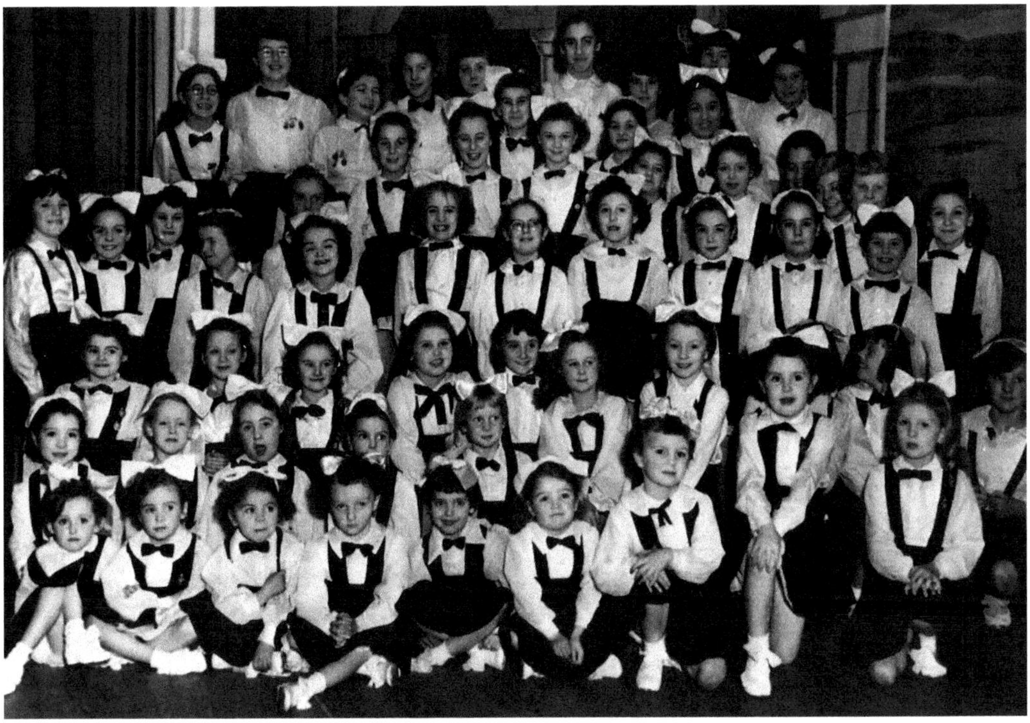

Dance Class
Mrs Jacob's dance class at St Kilda's church hall, Ellison Street.

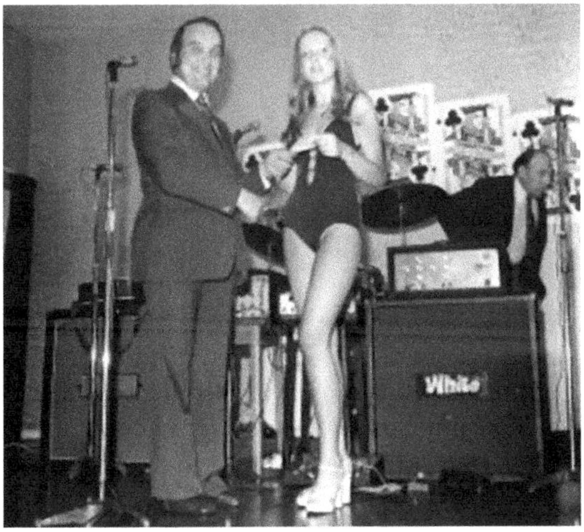

Jack O' Clubs
Local journalist and charitable fundraiser Jack Amos was responsible for writing the popular Jack O' Clubs column for the *Sunday Sun* newspaper. The Jack O' Clubs Sunday Roadshow travelled the region showcasing the club lifestyle of the North East. Jack is pictured here with Miss Clubland, Debbie Davis, at the Neon Social Club in April 1975.

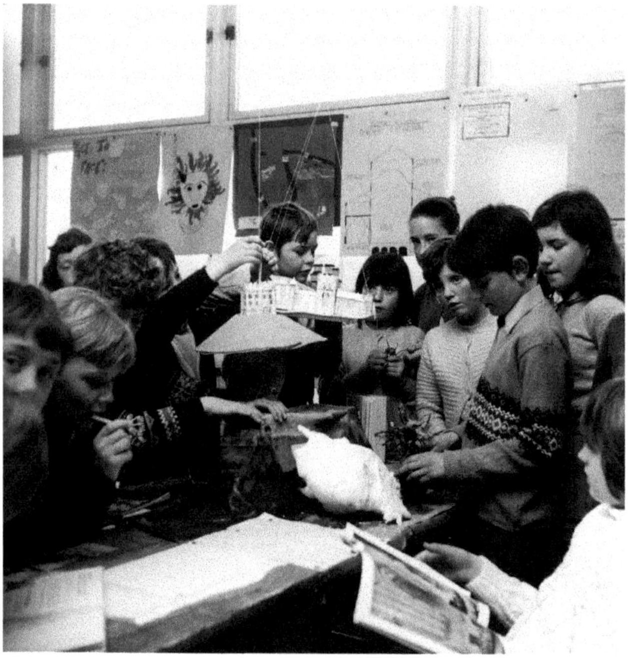

Dunn Street School

Pupils from Dunn Street school enjoying their new surroundings in July 1971.

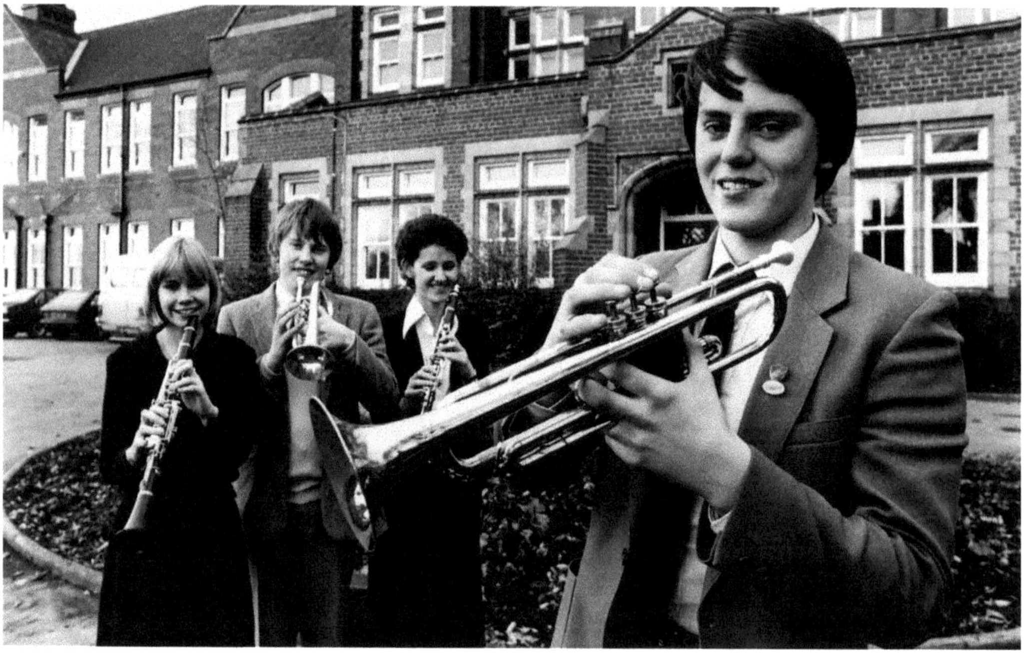

Springfield Comprehensive School

Springfield was formerly called Jarrow Grammar School. It became a comprehensive school in 1975, and the original building in Field Terrace, dating from 1911, was demolished in 2010 and replaced with a more modern establishment under the name of Jarrow School, Engineering Excellence in Education. Pictured: Young musicians in the grounds of the former grammar school in 1983.

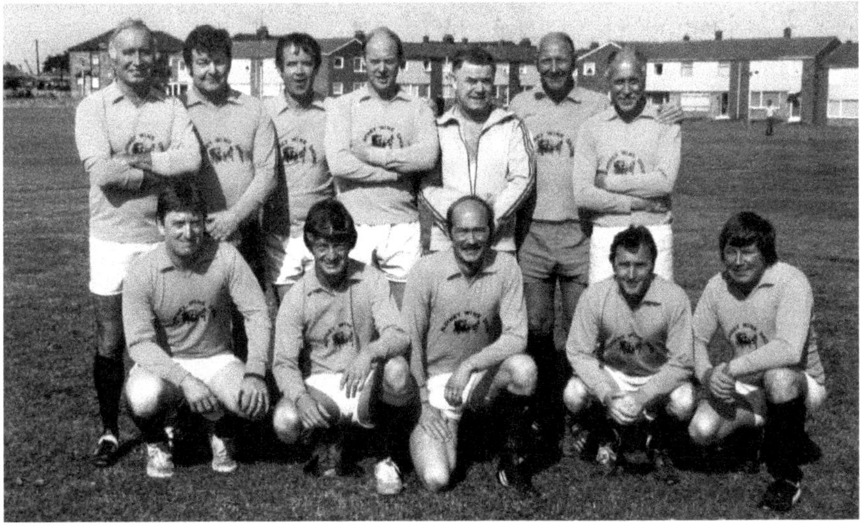

St Bede's Over 35s Football Team

This photograph of St Bede's football team for over 35s was taken around 1985 on the playing fields to the rear of the Clock Hotel at Hebburn, where local teams would play charity matches on bank holidays against rival senior teams from social clubs around the area. Among the people on this 1980s photograph are Joe Anthony, Terry McCullough, Ray Brown, Eddie McIntyre and Michael Joyce.

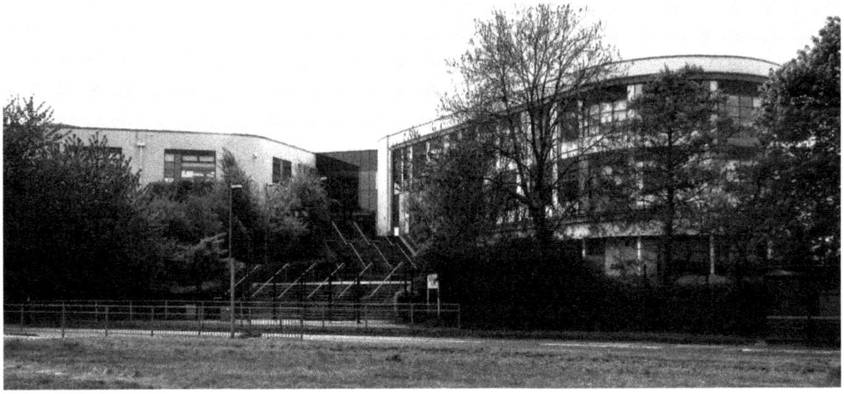

Jarrow School

The former Jarrow Grammar School building in Field Terrace was built in 1911, serving the town for almost a century until it ceased to maintain its status as a grammar school around 1975, changing its name to Springfield Comprehensive School after the merging of the Springfield and Hedworthfield Schools. From then, and still occupying the former school buildings, it became known as Jarrow School. The original school buildings were eventually demolished in 2010, after a replacement school building became available in Field Terrace, large enough to accommodate up to 900 students, and it rose to the heights of a specialist engineering college. The grounds of the former grammar school were developed into a comprehensive sports facility and swimming pool.

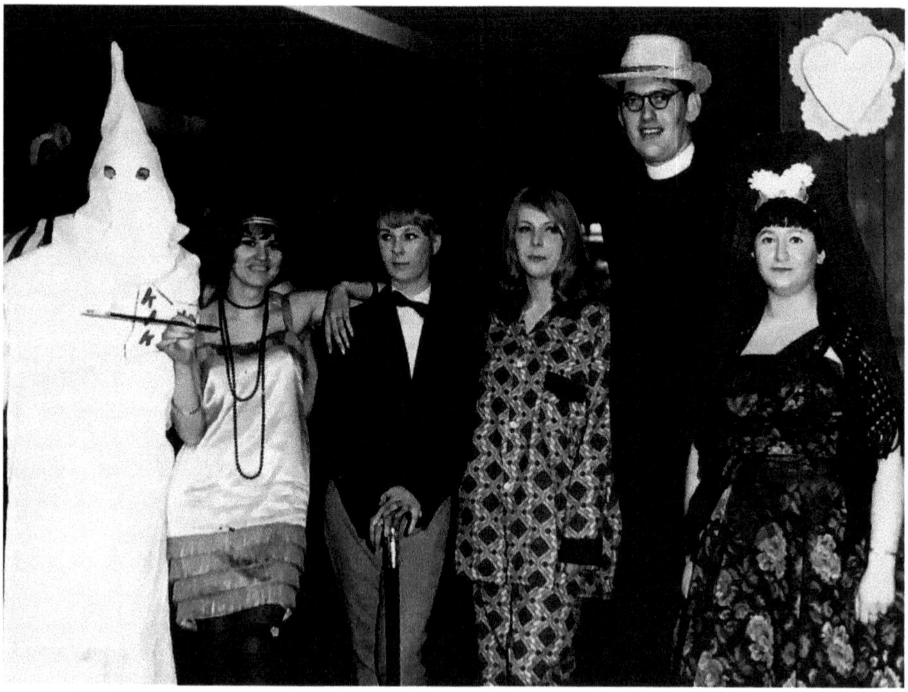

Excel Tenpin Bowling Centre

Above and below: Within the Excel Tenpin Bowling Centre there was an exclusive private lounge for the centre's members and guests. The licenced venue, independent from the bowling facilities, was organised by an annually elected committee who provided a resident band and entertainment throughout the year. Pictured: Valentine's Day fancy dress ball from 1966, and the ladies' bowling league from 1964.

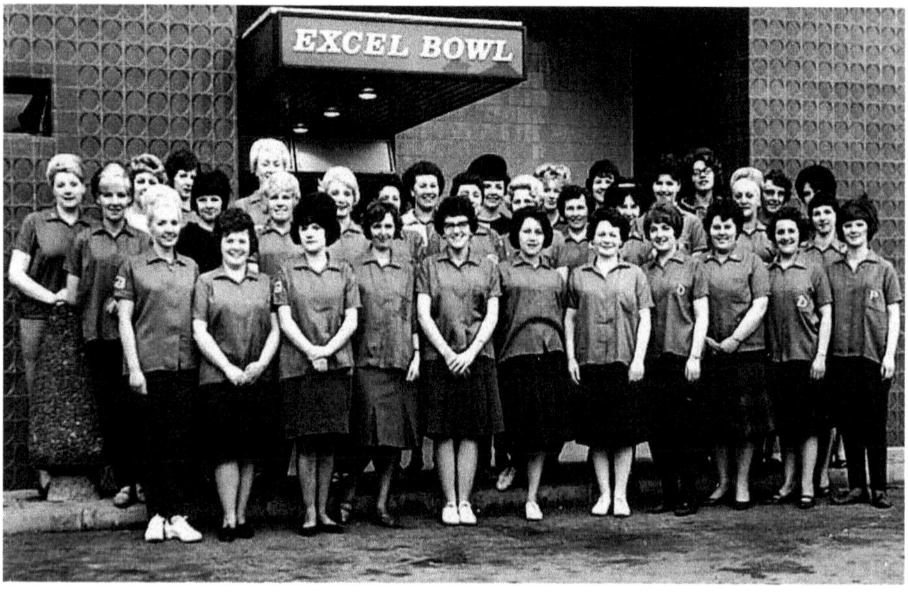

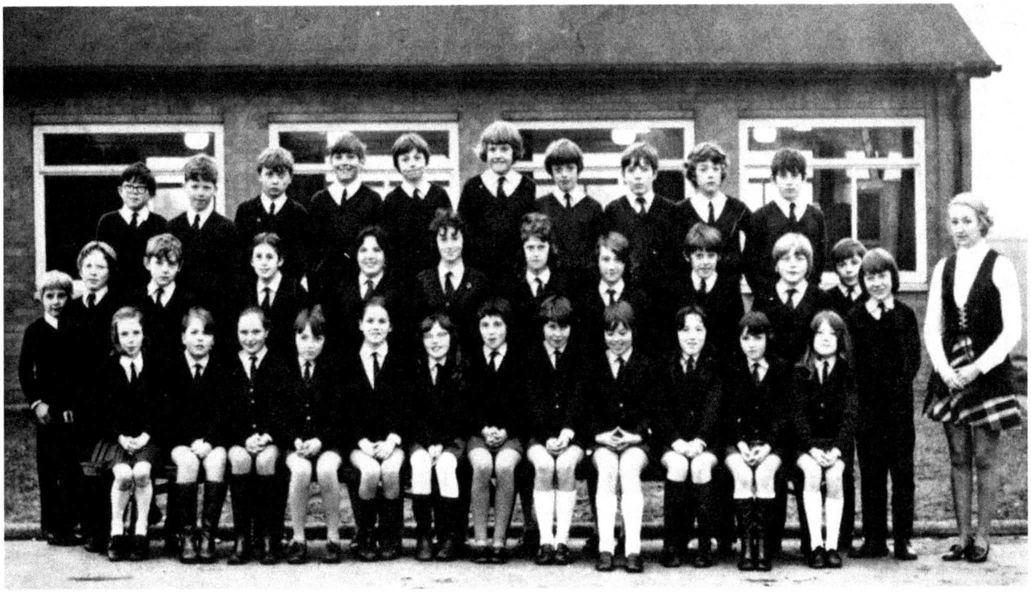

Belsfield School, Bede Burn Road, 1971.

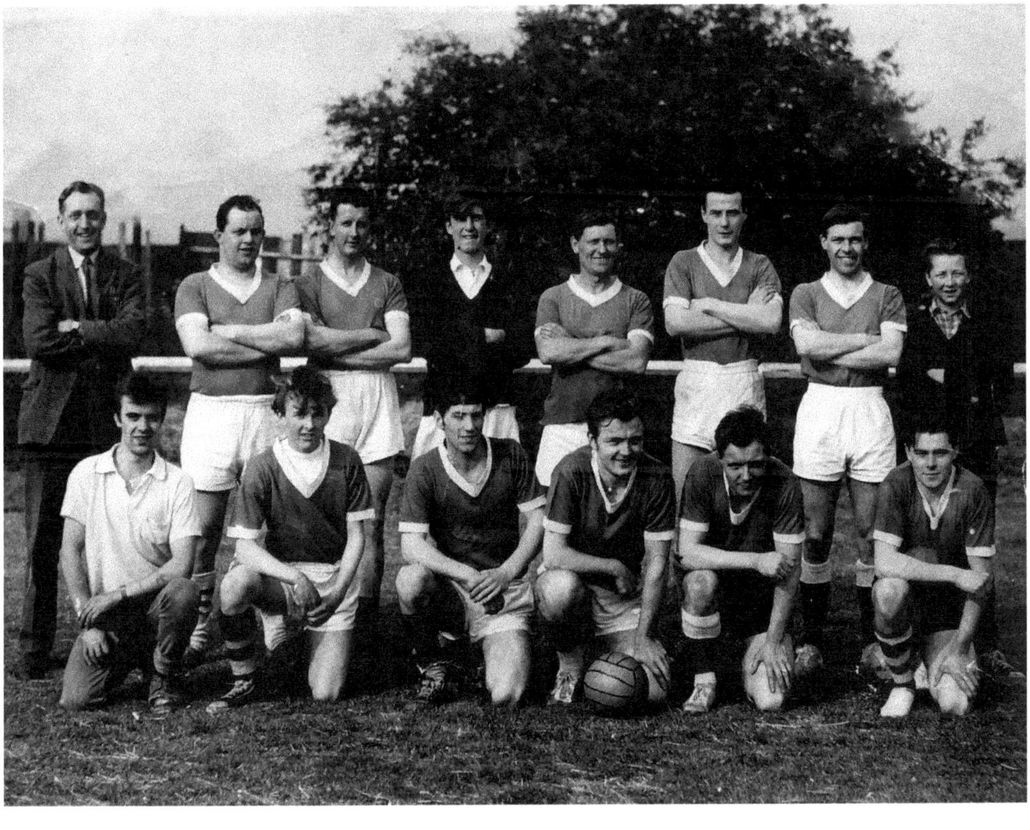

Armstrong Whitworth Football Team, 1965.

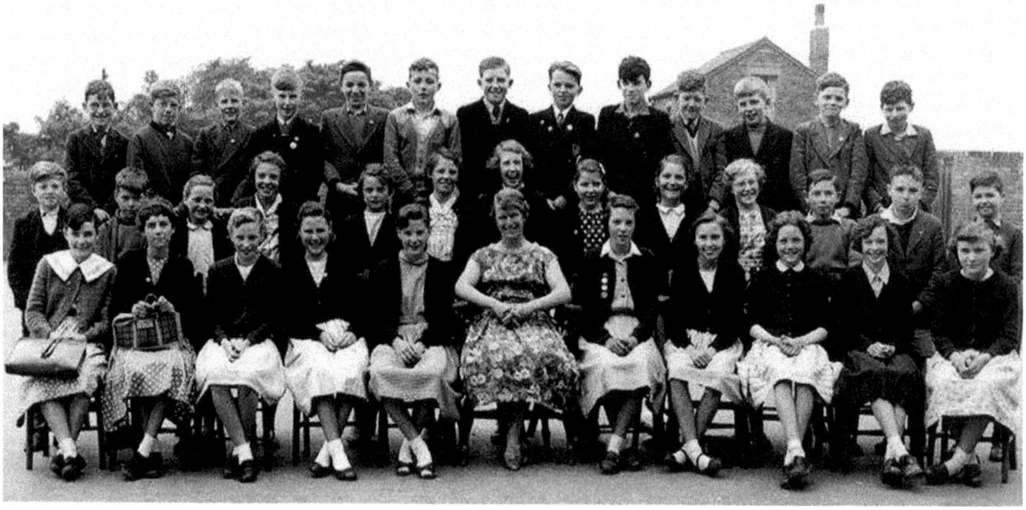

Central School class group from 1970.

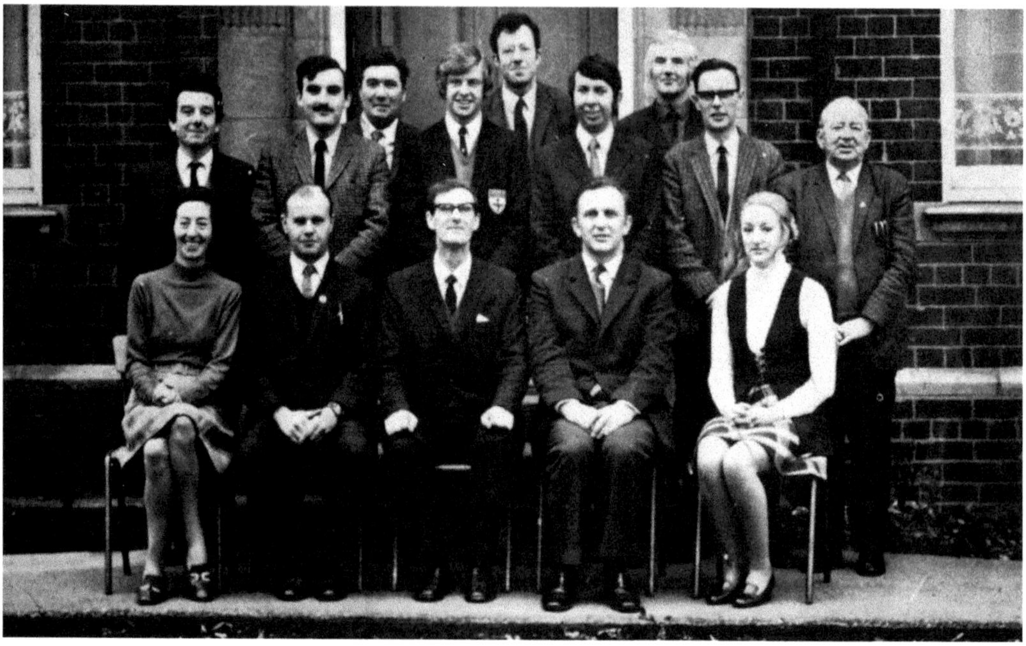

Belsfield School teaching staff from 1971.

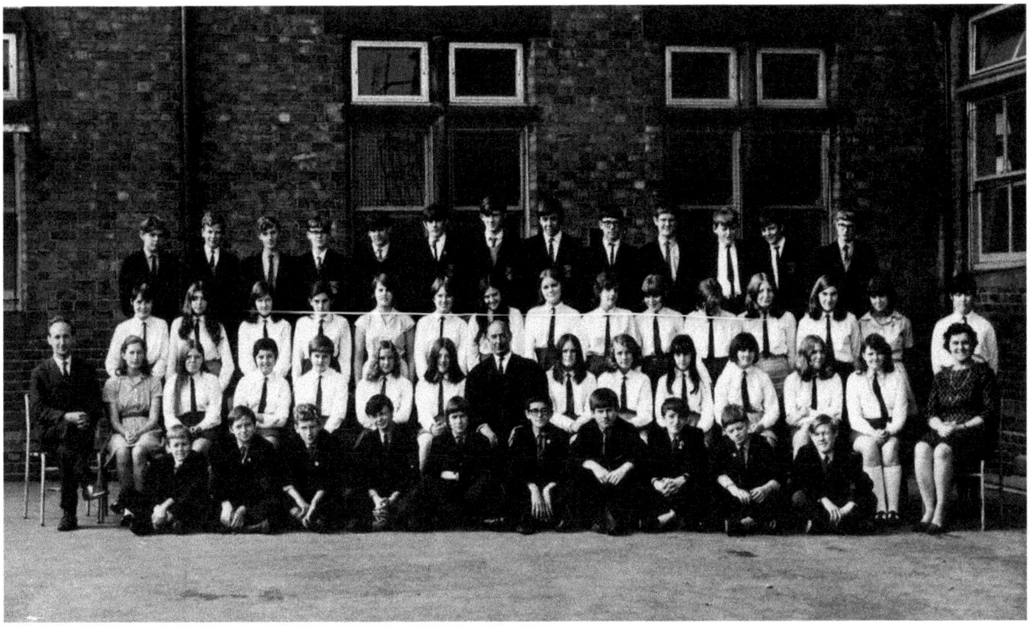

Central School class group from 1970.

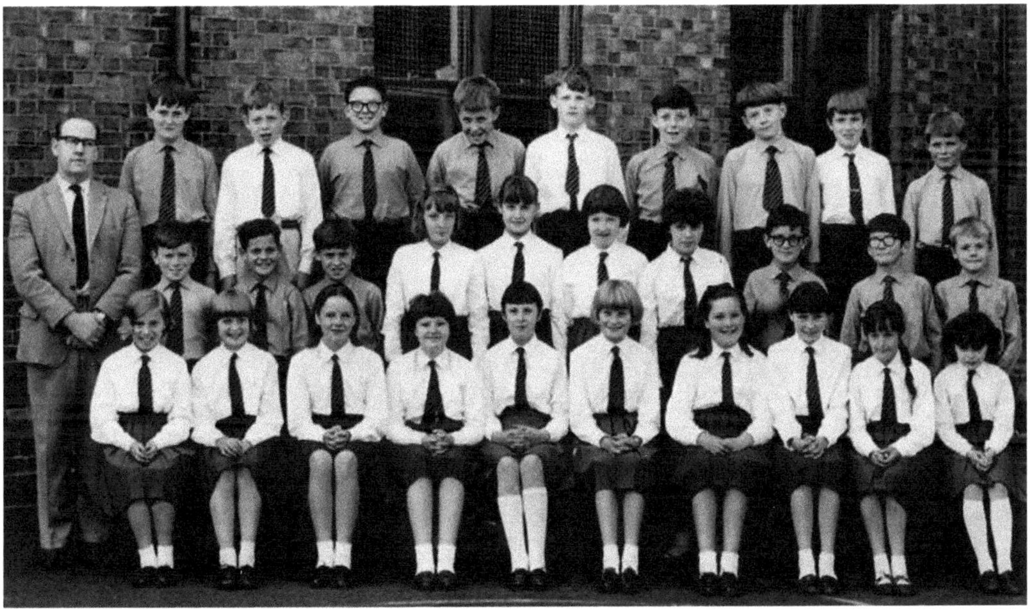

Central School class group from 1961.

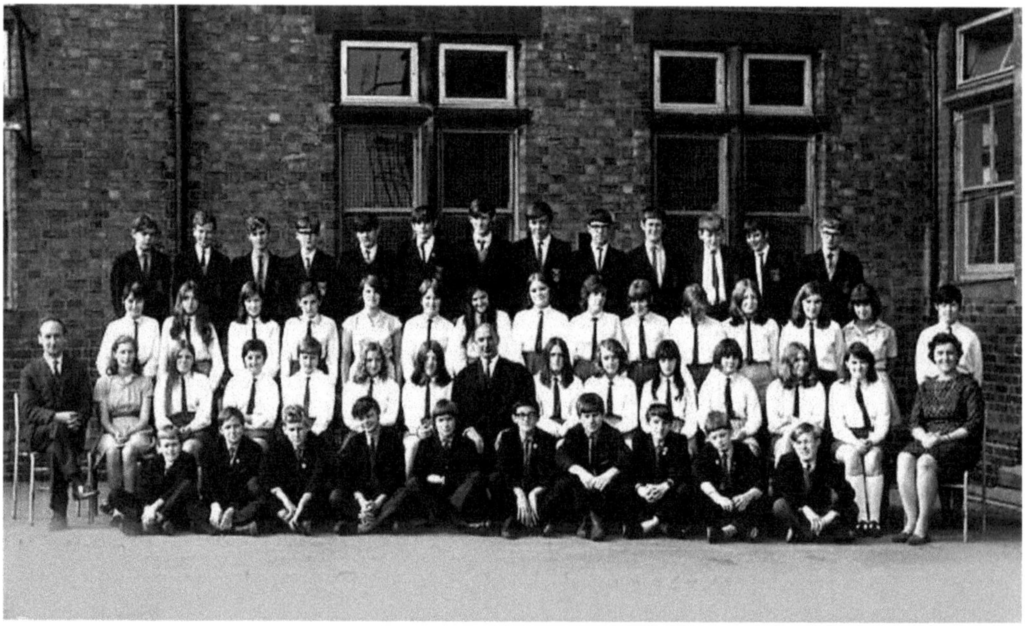

Central School class group from 1967.

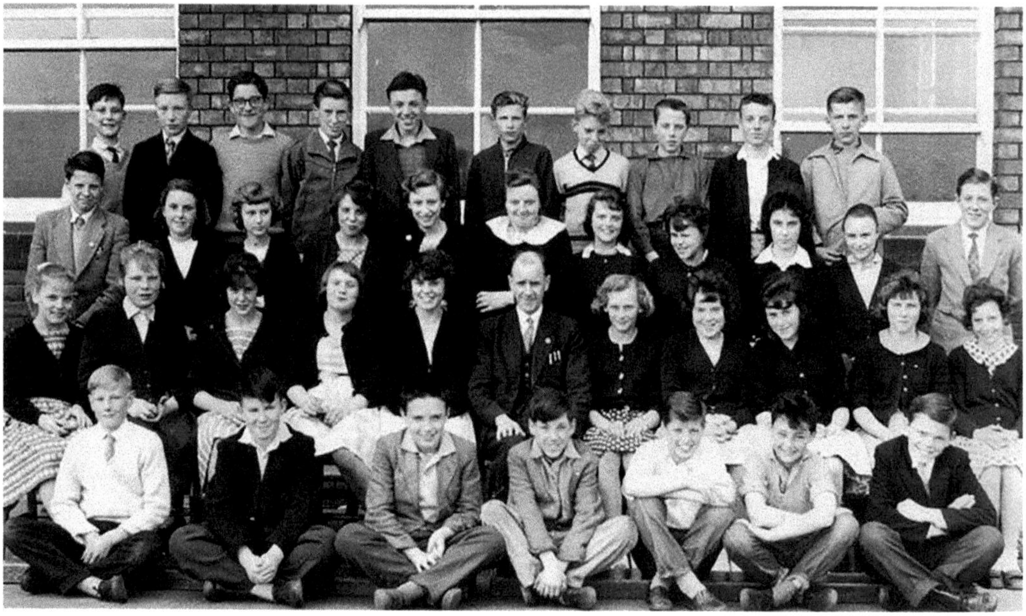

Croft Terrace C of E School class group from 1961.

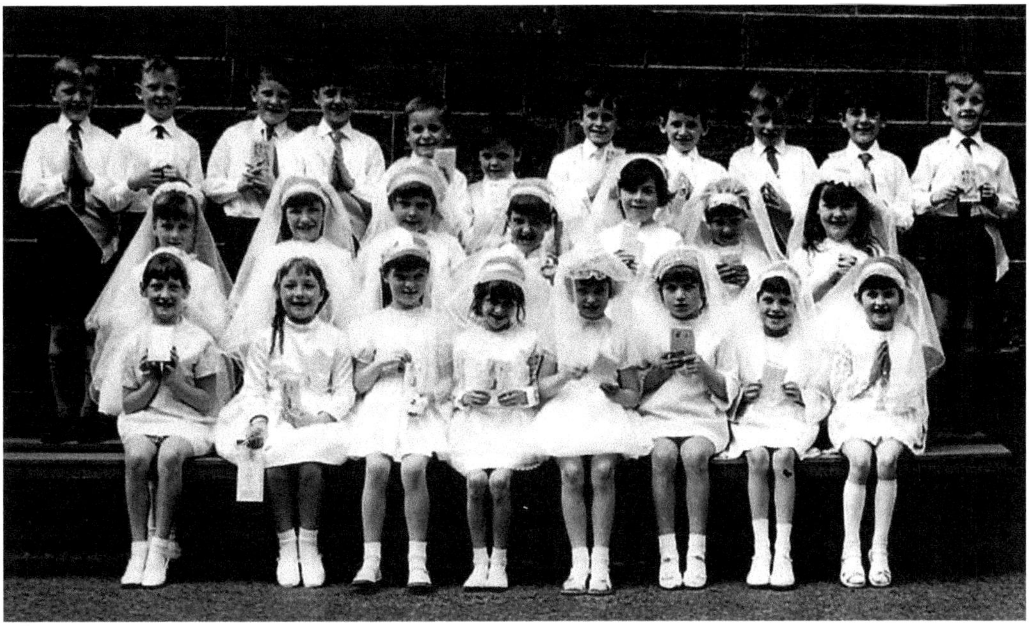

St Bede's Communicants from 1970.

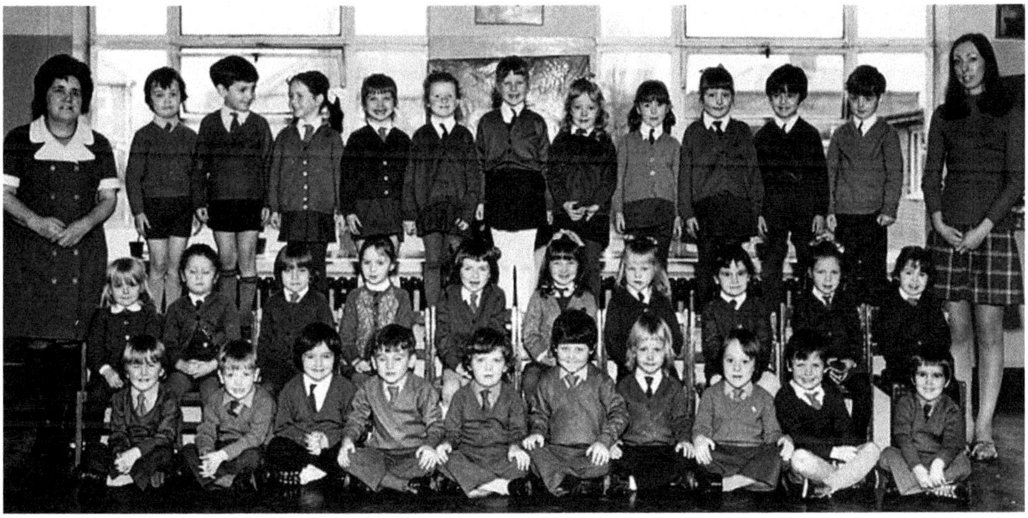

St Matthew's School class group from 1974.

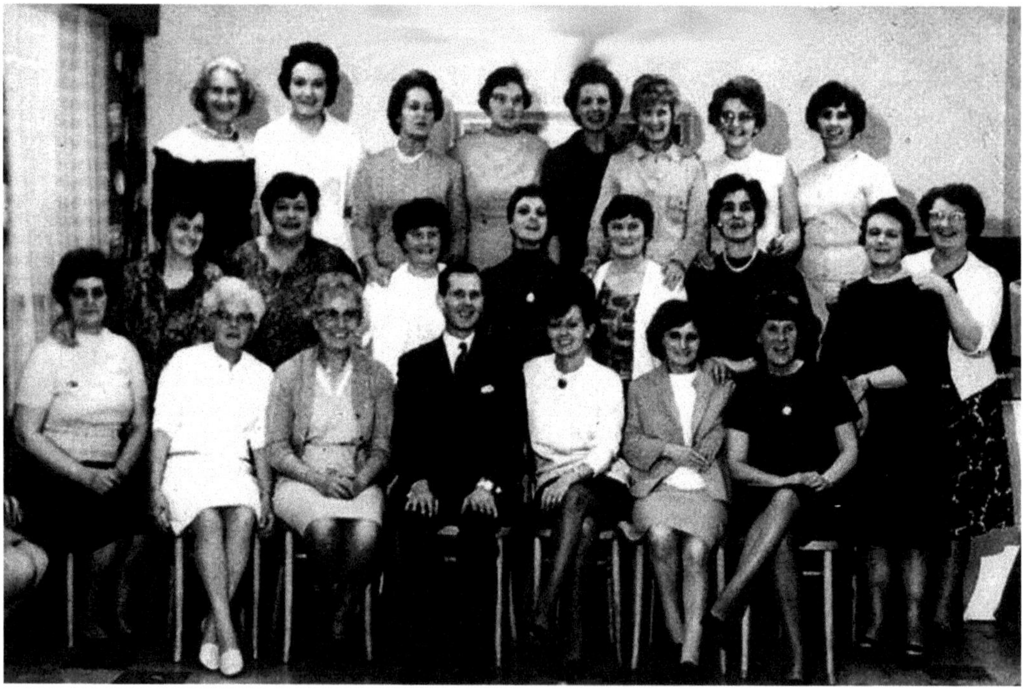

Woolworth Jarrow branch annual staff photograph from 1964.

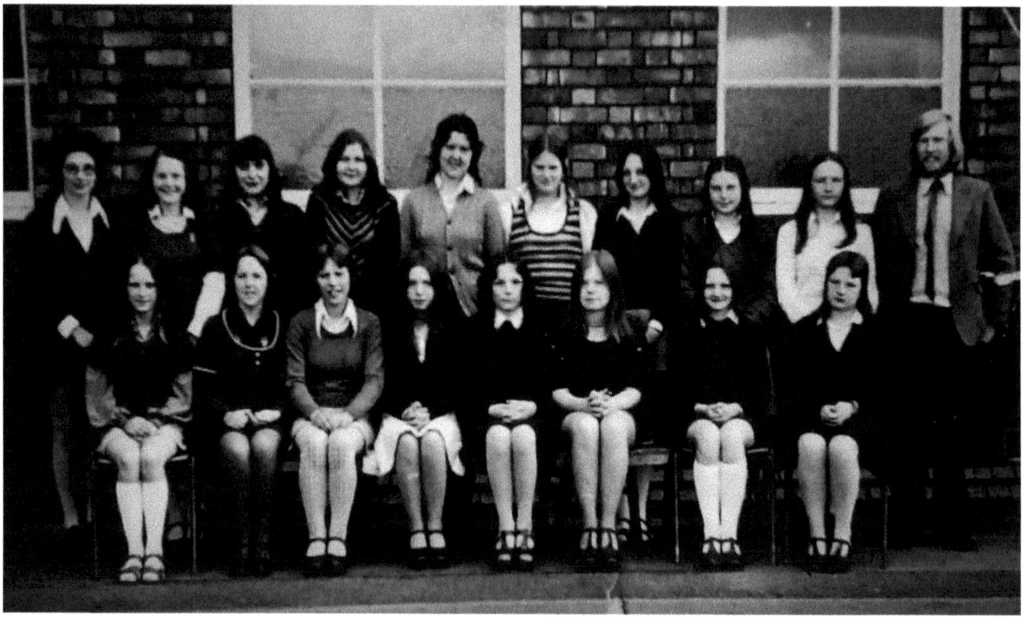

Croft Terrace School class group from 1974.

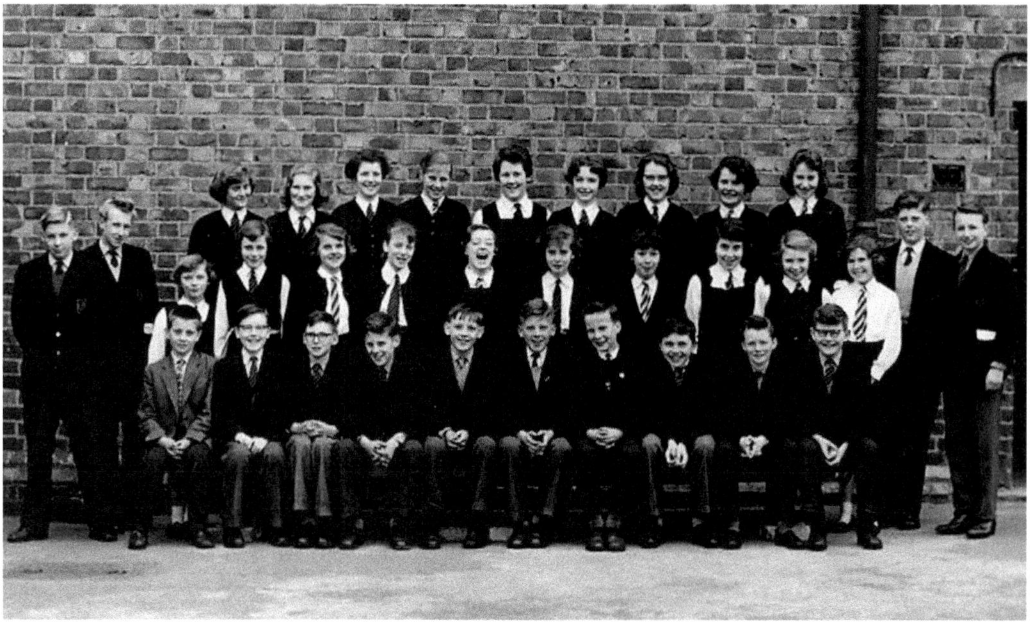

Above: Central School, 1960.

Right: Children Playing at Clervaux Nursery School, Jarrow.

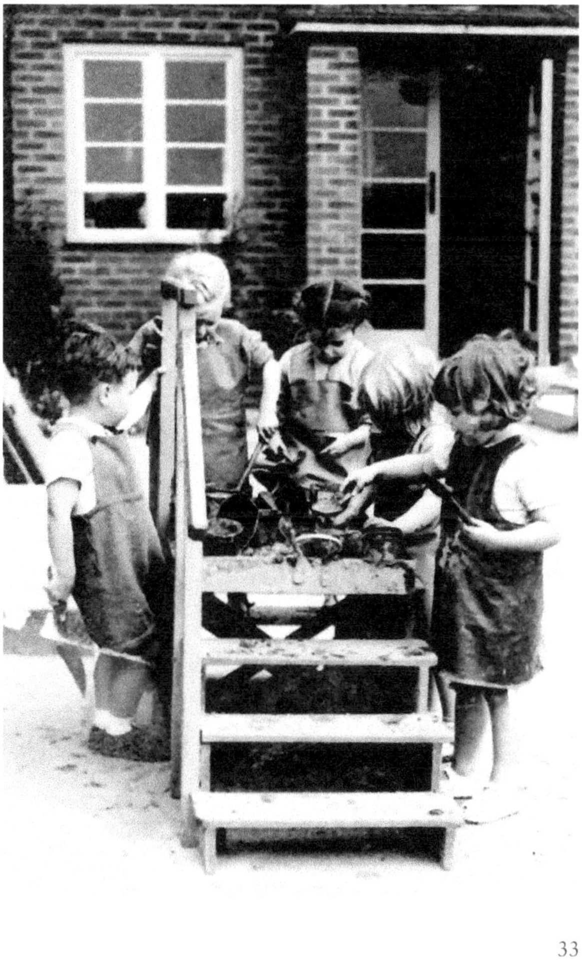

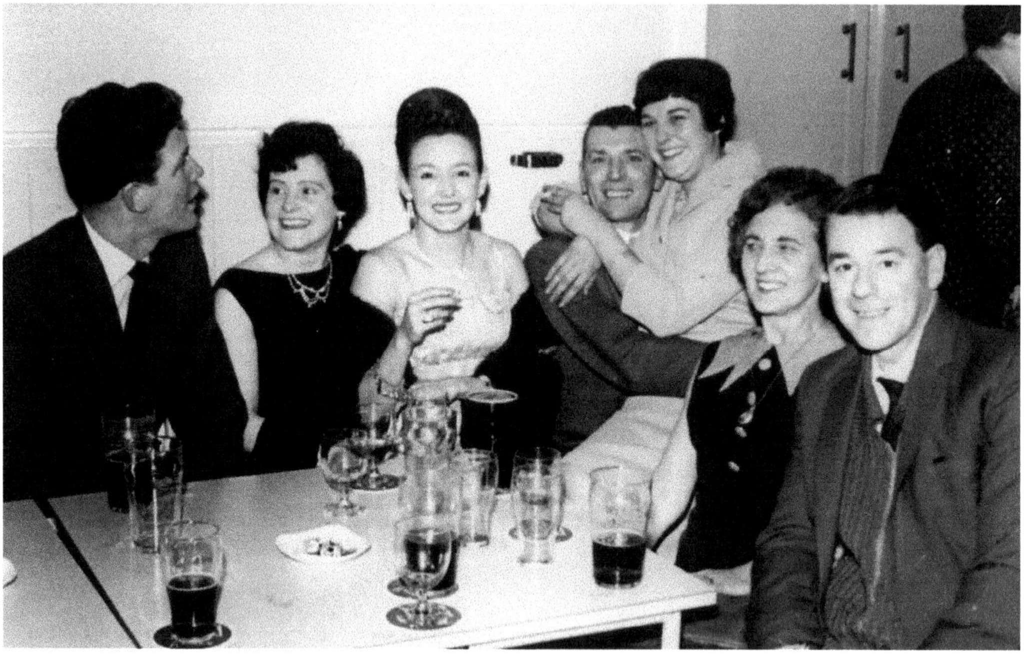

Woolworths Christmas party, Jarrow, 1963.

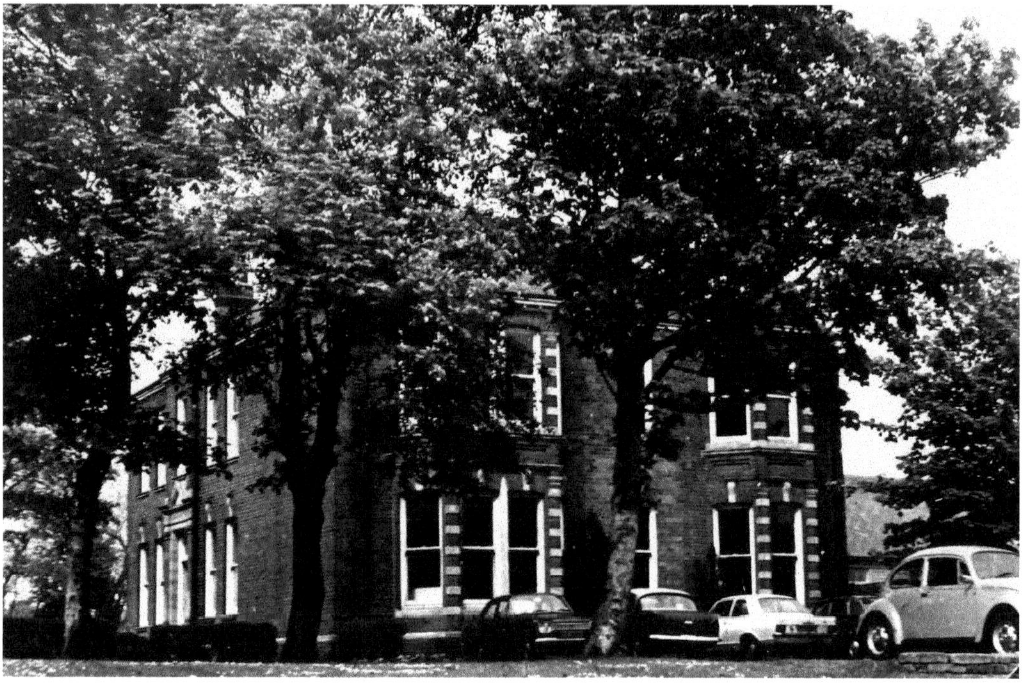

Belsfield School, 1972.

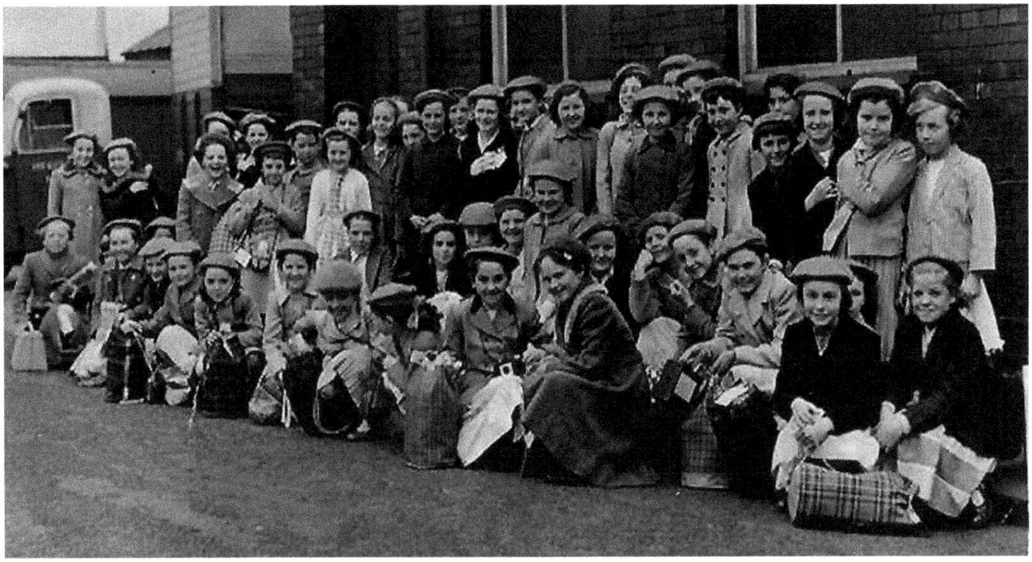

St Bede's Girls at Jarrow railway station preparing for a trip to London.

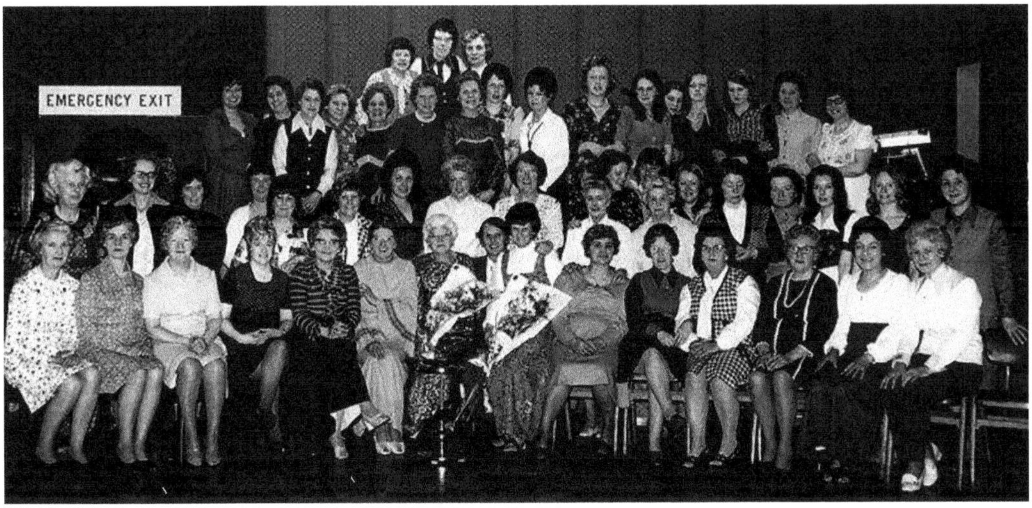

Woolworths annual staff photograph, Jarrow, from 1963.

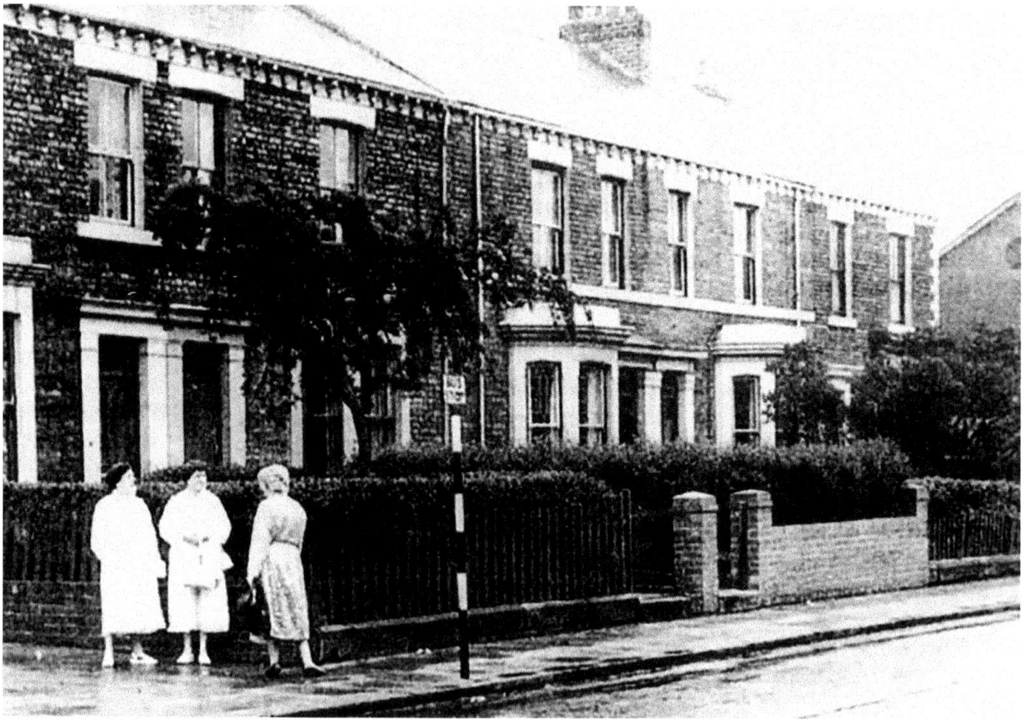

Albert Road, 1960.

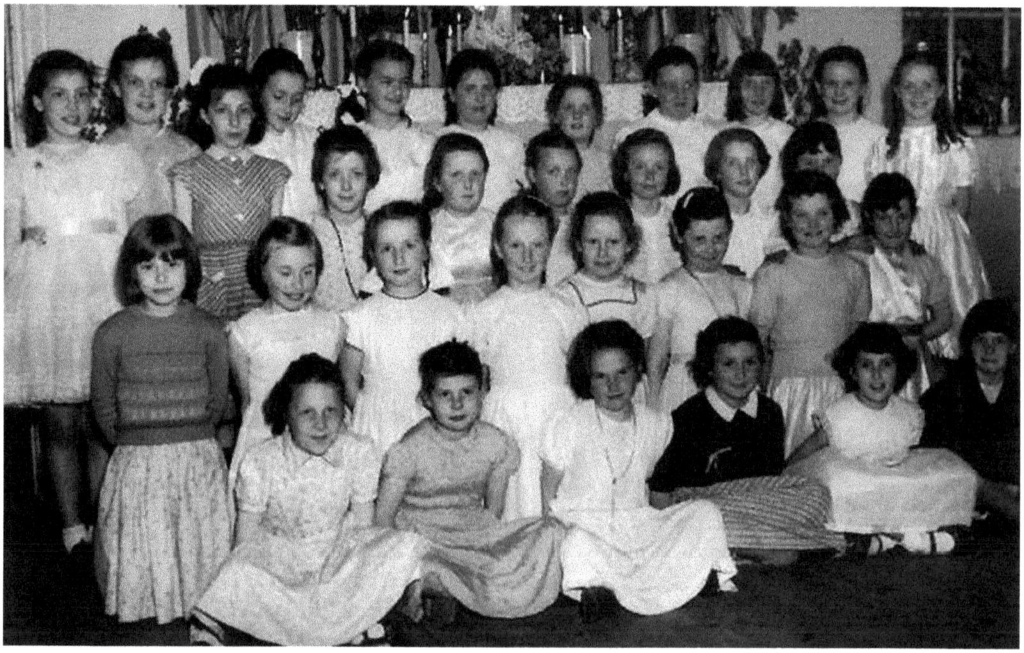

St Bede's girls.

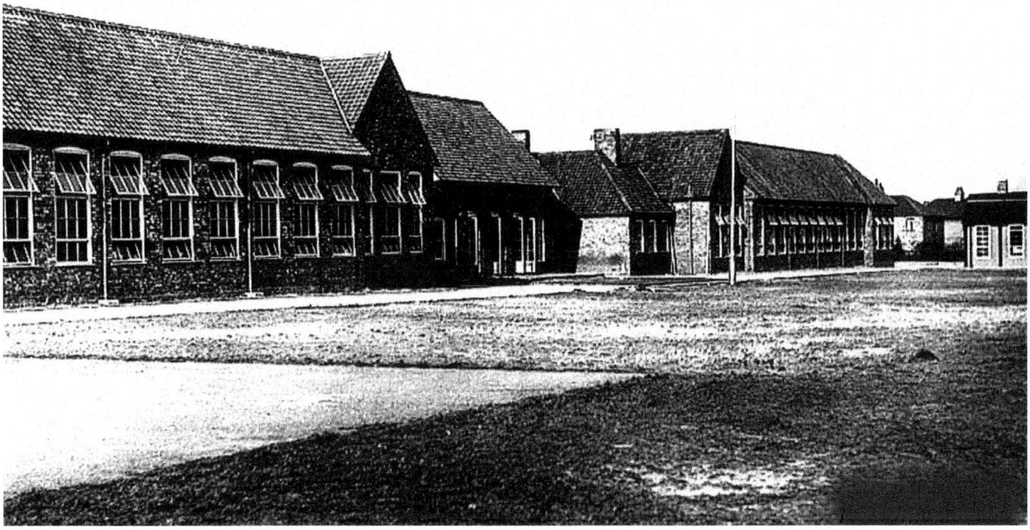

Valley View Infant & Junior School, 1962.

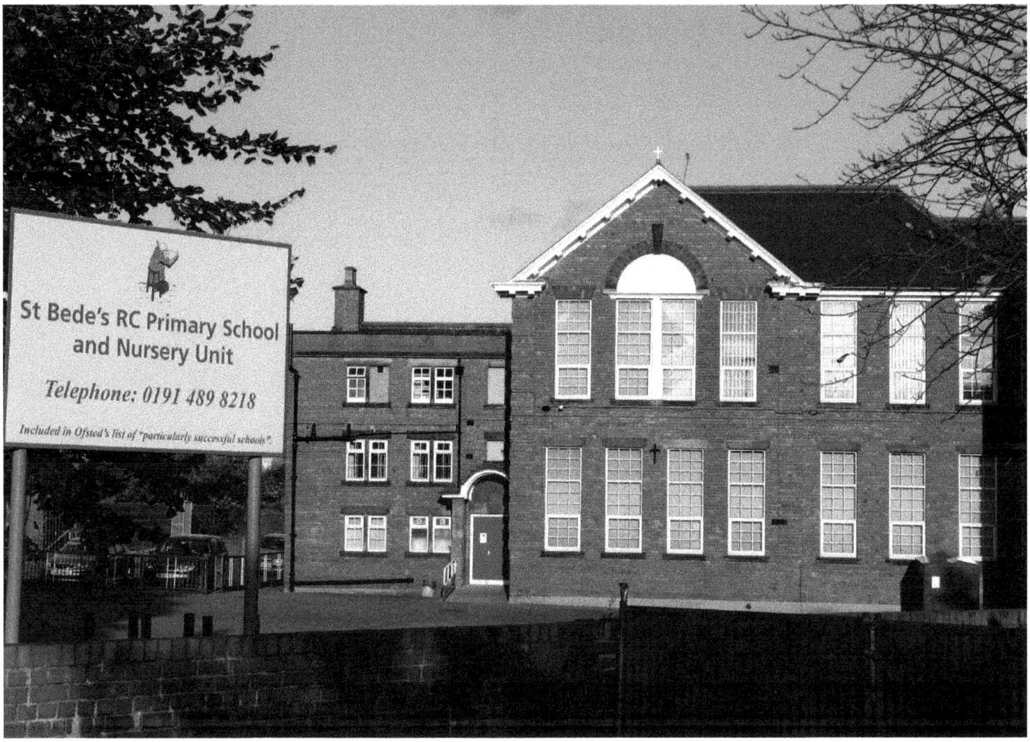

St Bede's School, Harold Street.

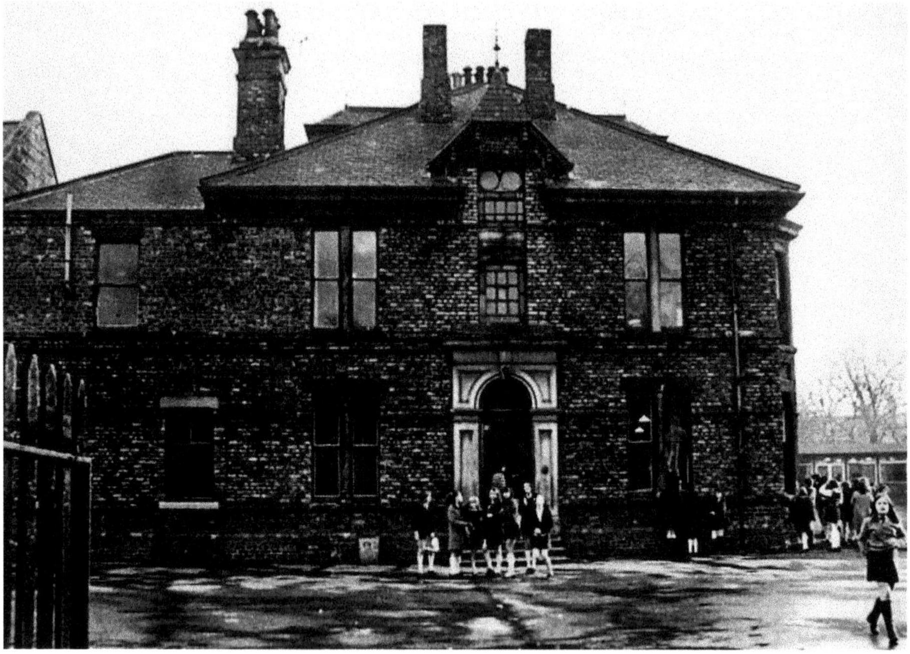

Mayfield Girls' School

Durham County Education Committee redeveloped two rather large residences on Pine Street, converting them into an education facility, creating Mayfield RC Girls' School in 1928. After a procession throughout Jarrow, a thanksgiving mass was offered prior to the opening ceremony. The school remained active for close to half a century as a Roman Catholic school for girls, until it was demolished during the 1970s.

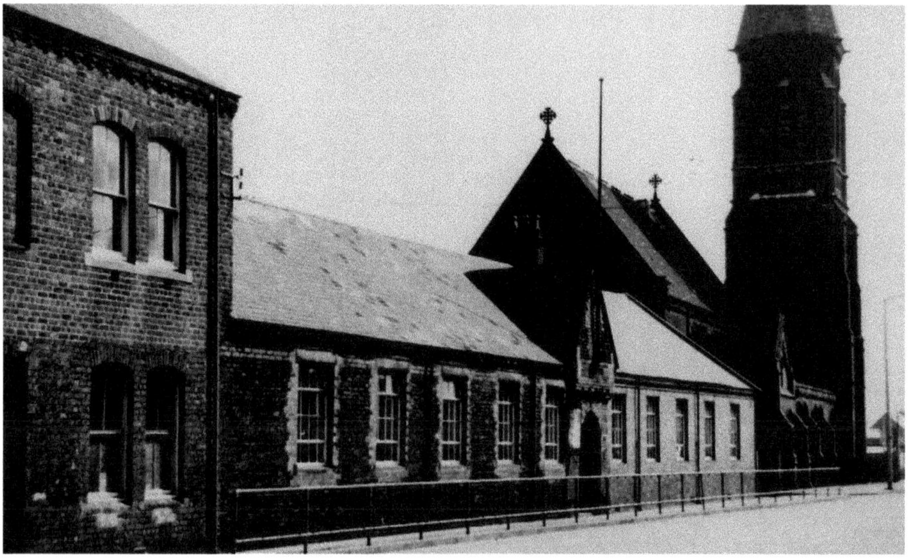

St Peter's Church and School, 1963.

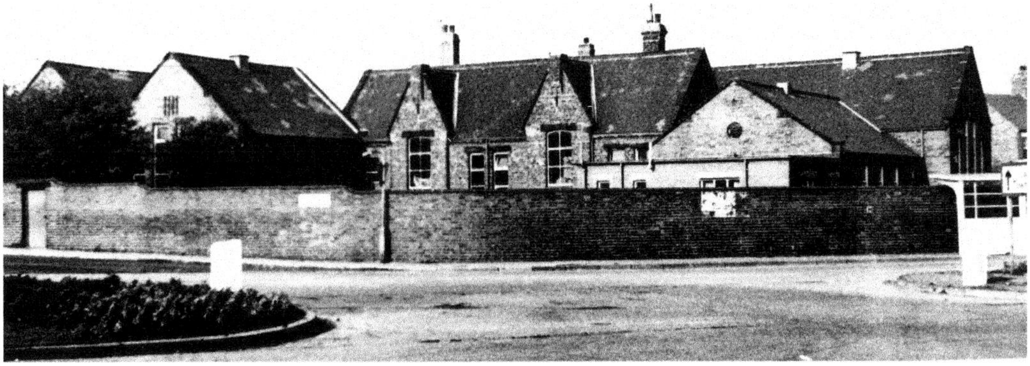

Bede Burn School, 1962.

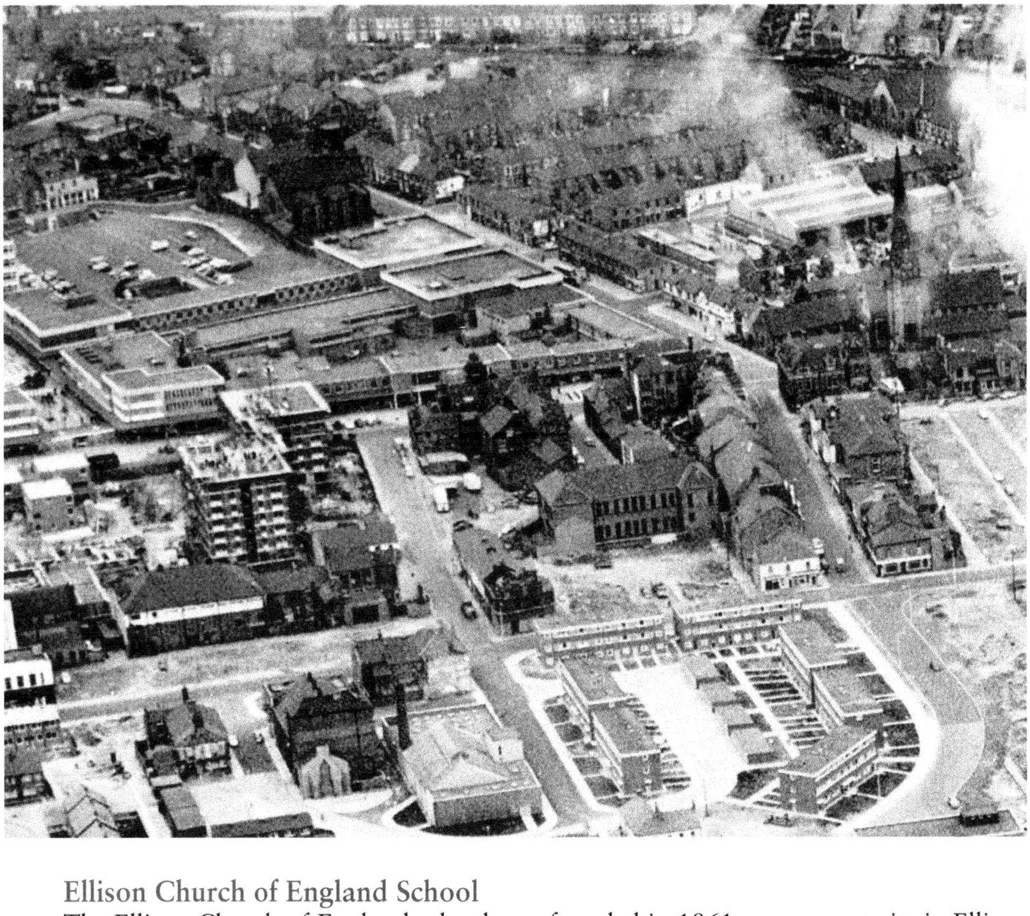

Ellison Church of England School

The Ellison Church of England school was founded in 1861 on a vacant site in Ellison Street. The purpose-built building was opened by its benefactors Sir Walter and Lady James. The second school was constructed close to the original and opened to the first influx of pupils in 1882. This building was demolished in the late 1970s and replaced with a more modern facility on Borough Road, amalgamating with St Peter's and forming Jarrow Cross Primary School. Pictured: an aerial view of the second school from 1964.

REGENERATION AND HOUSING

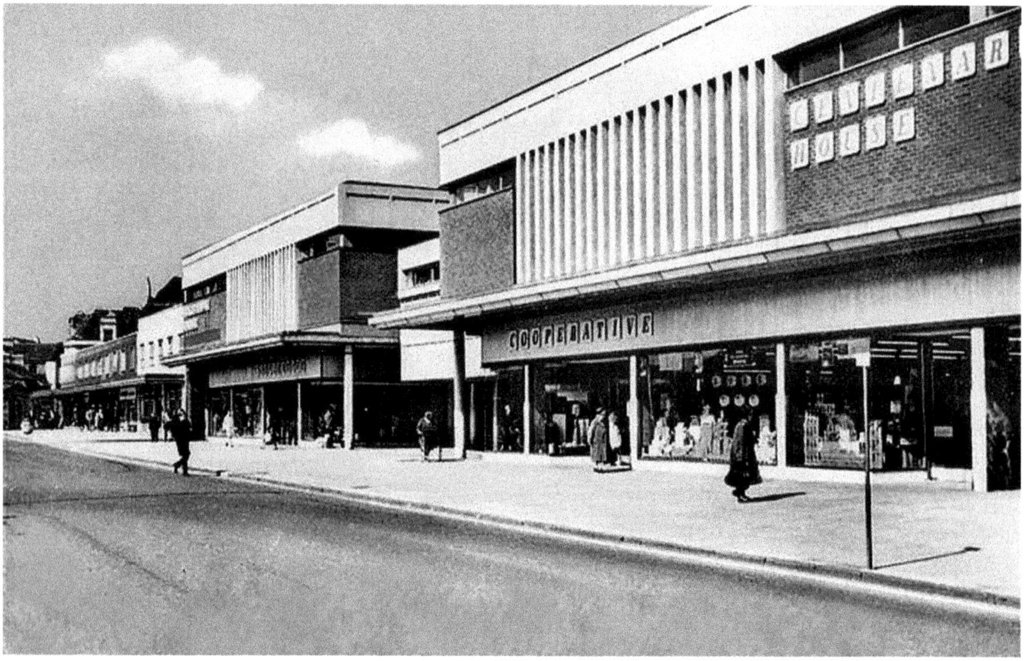

Centenary House

Above and opposite above: The security of work in Jarrow meant families looked to the future with confidence. With this security came a variety of prospects and a better standard of living, enabling many to afford the modern conveniences now on offer on the High Street. With their new-found wealth, families, together with the convenience of hire purchase agreements, were able to afford the luxury of televisions, washing machines and refrigerators. The availability and affordability of the easy payment plans offered by the agreements transformed the lives of millions of families nationwide, freeing up time for leisure activities. For Jarrow folk, white goods, as they became known were available in several outlets within the town centre, offering terms favourable to most budgets. Pictured: Jarrow & Hebburn Co-operative Society department store at Centenary House in the town centre.

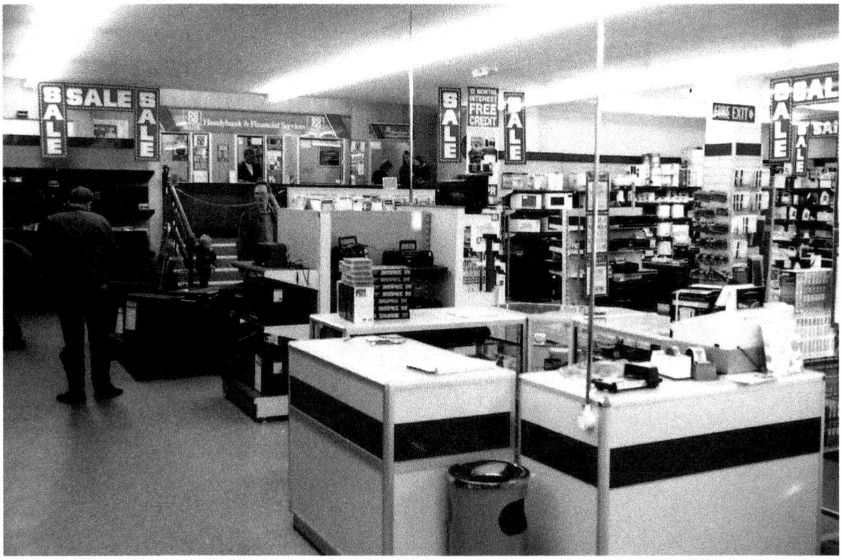

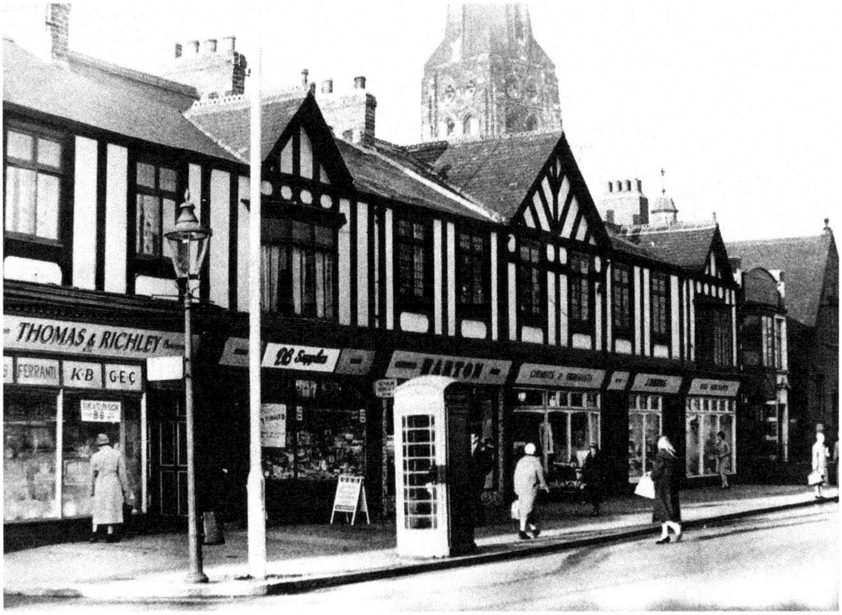

Ellison Street

The must-have gismo for teenagers during the 1960s was without doubt the transistor radio. This battery-powered, pocket-sized portable invention gave people the freedom to listen to music anywhere – or to anyone fortunate enough to own such a device. The popularity of the transistor was eventually superseded by more sophisticated devices with superior sound quality. The Walkman, a Japanese invention from Sony released in 1979, was a portable magnetic tape cassette player, designed to listen to music of your choice on the move, which eventually progressed to the CD player. The principal suppliers of such merchandise in Jarrow were Steinmeyer House in Bede Precinct and Thomas & Richley, pictured here, in Ellison Street.

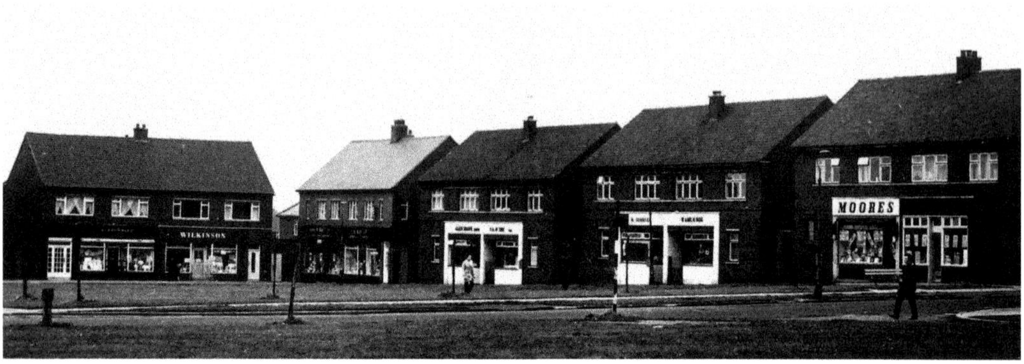

South Leam Estate

The mass exodus from Jarrow town centre began in earnest around 1956, with the occupation of the recently completed accommodation on the estate we know today as the Scotch Estate. These self-contained smart dwellings were a vast and welcome improvement to the living conditions endured by so many for so long in the back-to-back Victorian terraces, which were now being rapidly demolished. By 1960, the now-established Scotch Estate had a small but comprehensive assortment of shops situated on Edinburgh Road. This photograph of the shops was taken in 1970.

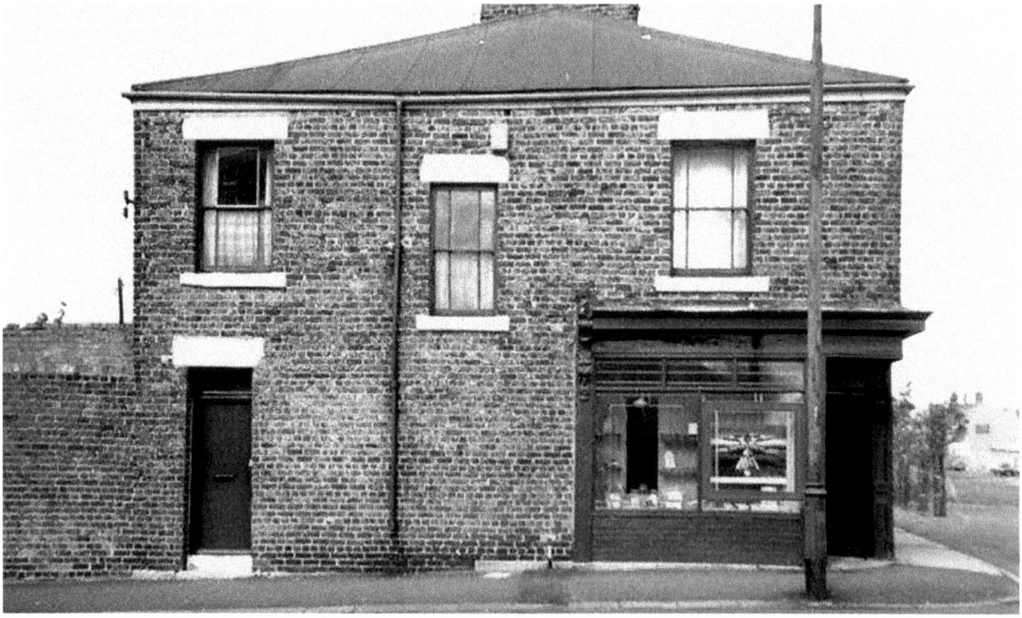

The Corner Shop

As Jarrow was selected by the Arndale Property Trust Company to be their flagship traffic-free commercial centre, the town still had an abundance of corner shops, purveying all manner of general goods and groceries. The word grocer is a derivation of the term 'grosser' that dates to the seventeenth century, when shopkeepers purchased produce by the gross. Today, independent grocers still tend to purchase by the gross and by the dozen. Pictured: Henry Mallen's General Dealers, Drury Lane, 1970.

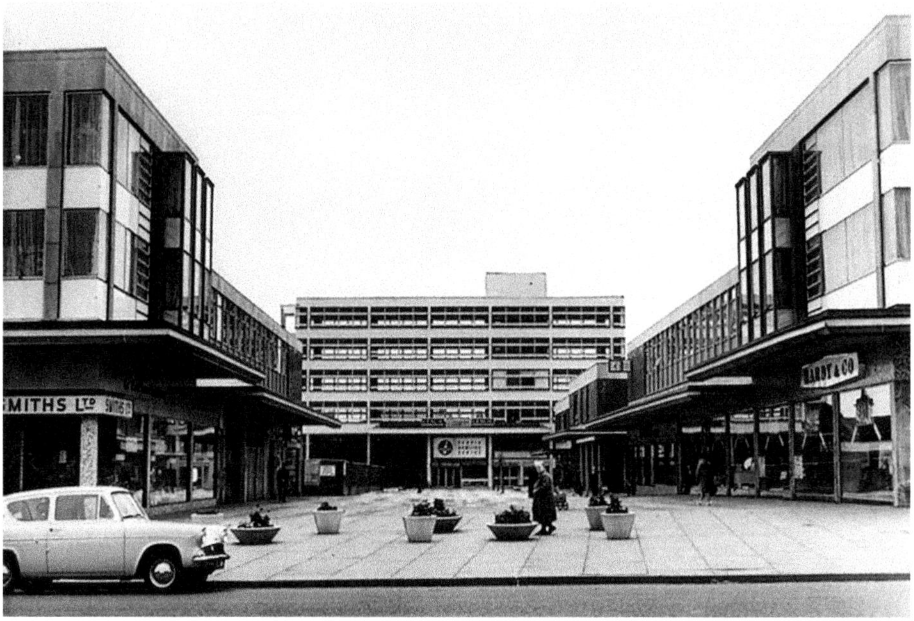

Arndale Centre

Above and below: The shopping precincts in the town centre bear little resemblance to when phase one of the innovative shopping experience began in 1961. The Arndale Centre, as it was known back then, was the work of the Arndale Property Trust Company, whose headquarters were in Manchester. The company was the merger of two businessmen, Arnold Hagenbach and Sam Chippindale, and it is from here the name Arndale was derived. Ownership of the Jarrow Centre has changed hands on several occasions and undergone varying stages of refurbishment in its sixty-year existence. Today, the centre is in the capable hands of Savills Property Development Company Ltd and is known as the Viking Centre.

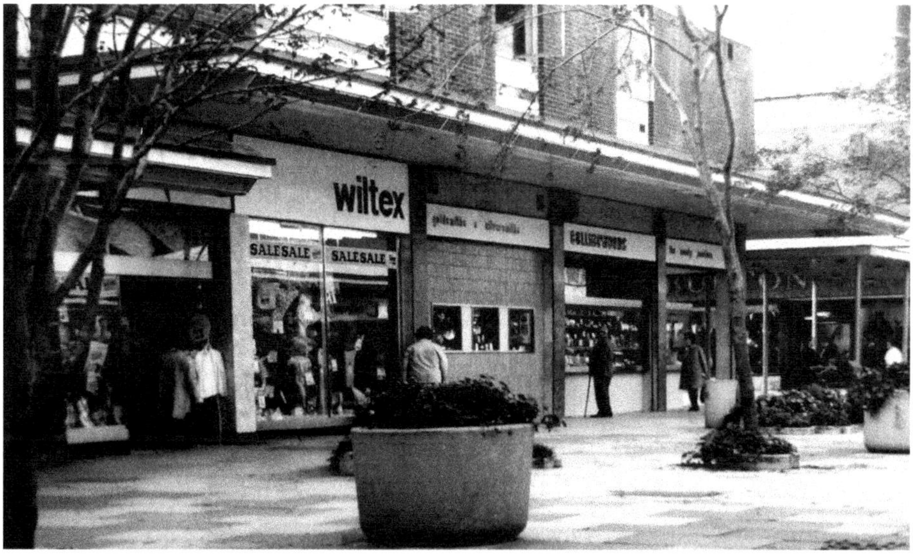

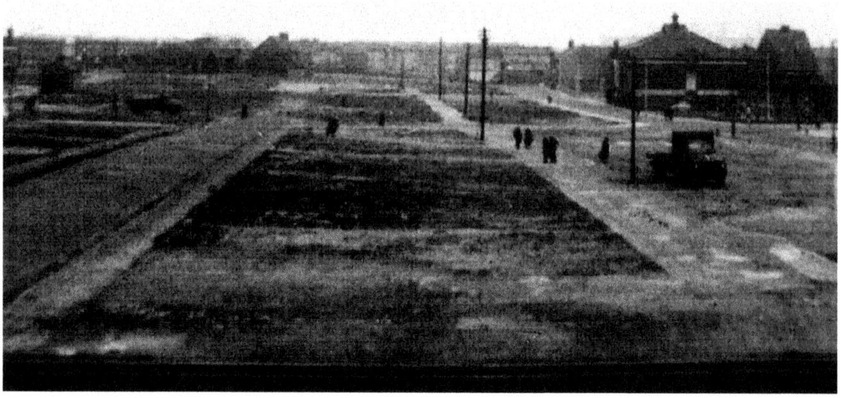

Market Square Clearance Site

The accompanying image of the Market Square clearance site, dated from around 1962, was a prime site right in the centre of town and a perfect spot for the development of modern housing. This unusual view was taken from the Town Hall, looking in an easterly direction, and typifies the size of the future development of municipal housing in North Court and Grange Court by Jarrow Council. The Regal Cinema is clearly visible to the right of the image, and the remains of South Street are evident to the left.

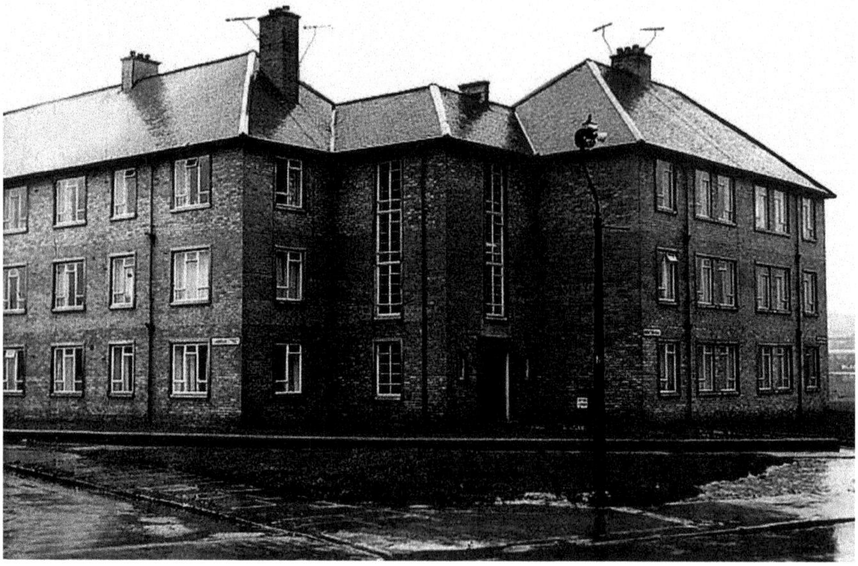

Festival Flats

Built in 1951 to commemorate the Festival of Britain, the troubled Festival Flats in High Street became a prime target for vandalism. The poorly designed housing complex of eighty-four flats was demolished in 1982, after a lifespan of just thirty-one years. Several attempts by the council to maintain and refurbish the former luxury accommodation back to their original condition were all unsuccessful, resulting in demolition being the most cost-effective solution. This photograph dates from 1970.

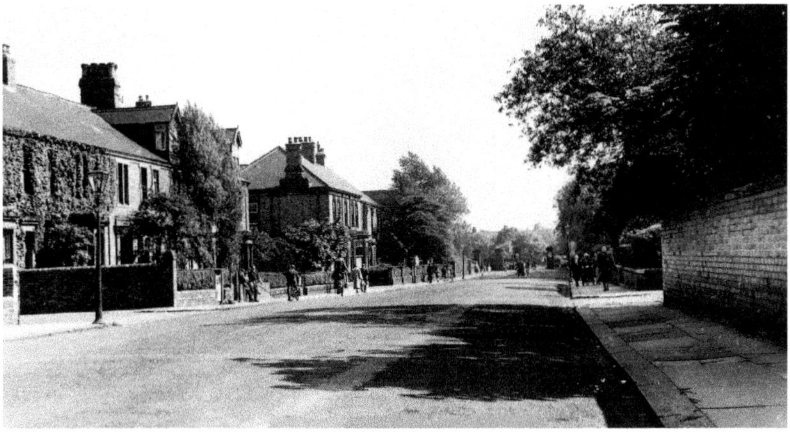

Park Road

The prestigious terrace houses to the left of the accompanying image of Park Road look as good today as they did when first built, which was towards the end of the nineteenth century. The imposing building in the centre of the image was the former Jarrow Trades & Labour Club, which was demolished and replaced with private housing.

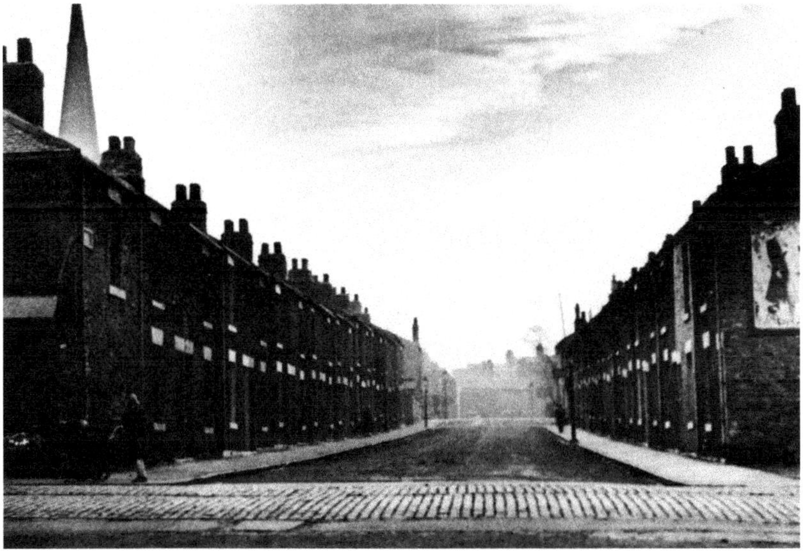

Clayton Street

The dimly lit, grimy terraced accommodation of Clayton Street, blackened with decades of sooty deposits from the chimneys of many of the region's industrial giants. These chimneys and deposits represented the heavy engineering works that once lined the banks of the River Tyne. The terraces were just a tiny proportion of accommodation that the town offered to the thousands of men who toiled twelve hours a day, seven days a week manning these industries while Jarrow enjoyed the prosperous years of shipbuilding. These terraces, along with many others, were demolished during the 1960s.

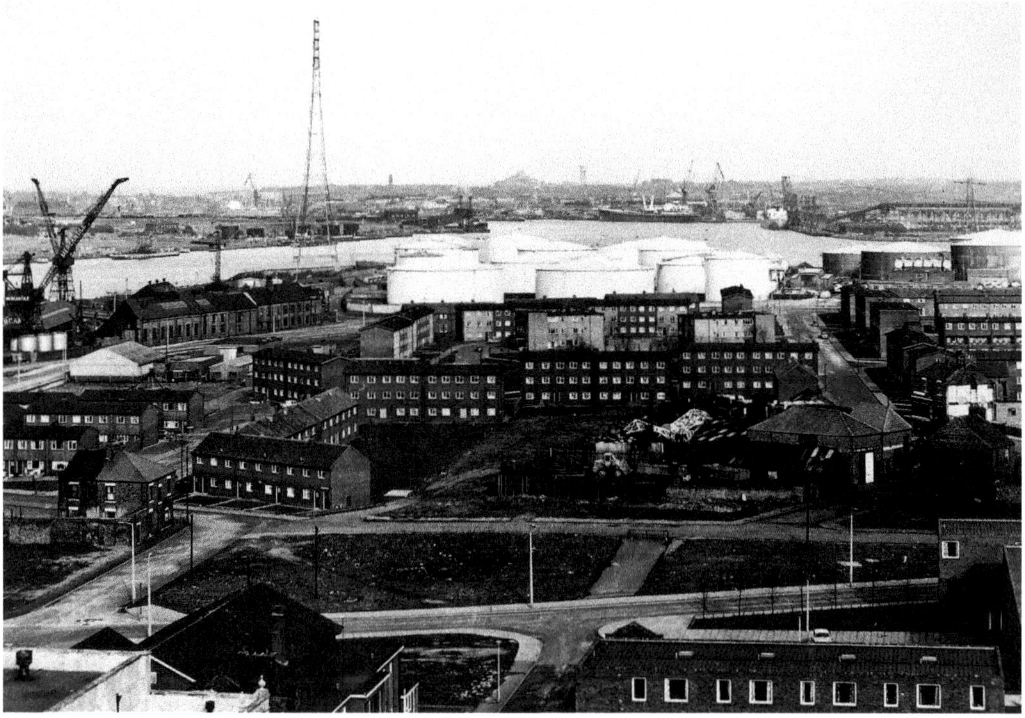

Queens Road Development

Above and below: Taken in 1962, this photograph captures the regeneration of accommodation in the town centre while under construction. In the foreground is the Jarrow Iron & Metal Co scrapyard in Pitt Street. The smart housing directly behind it is the result of the Queens Road development from the 1950s and 1960s. This accommodation was subject to a major restoration programme during the 1970s, as seen in the second image.

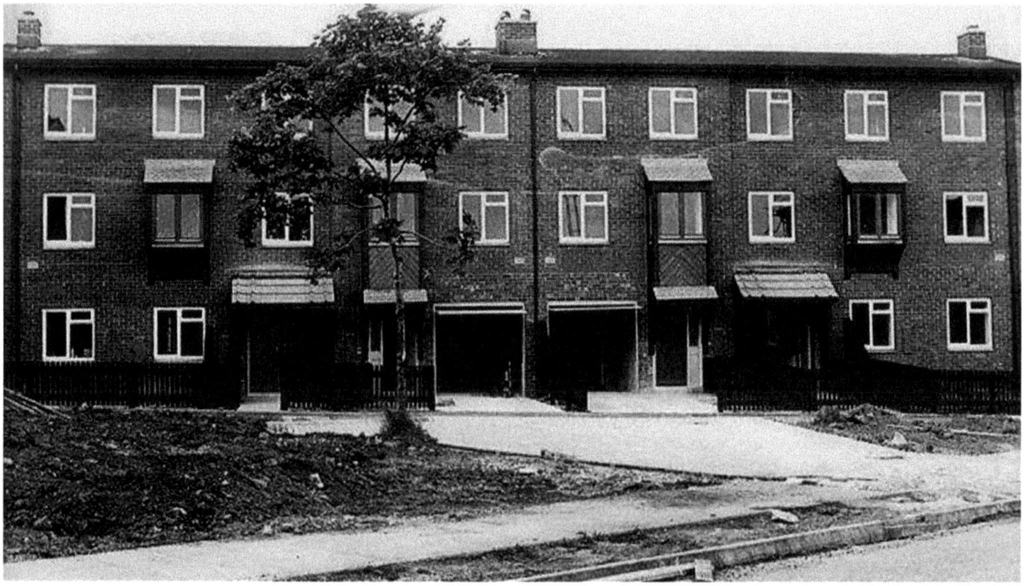

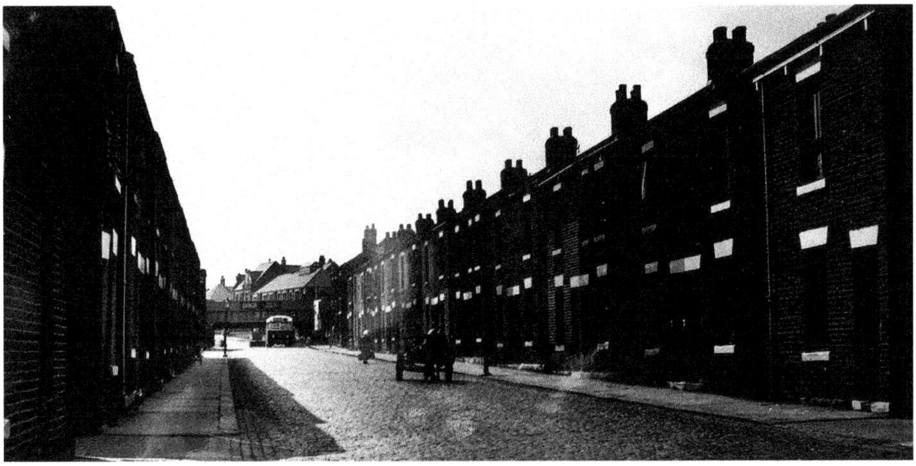

Palmer Street

The old gas lamps, cobblestones, flagged pavements, dimly lit terraces of houses and the absence of road markings that were characteristic of Palmer Street demonstrate what life was like up until the 1960s, when the accommodation was demolished and the town changed beyond recognition. Since the 1970s, the area has been occupied by a prosperous business park.

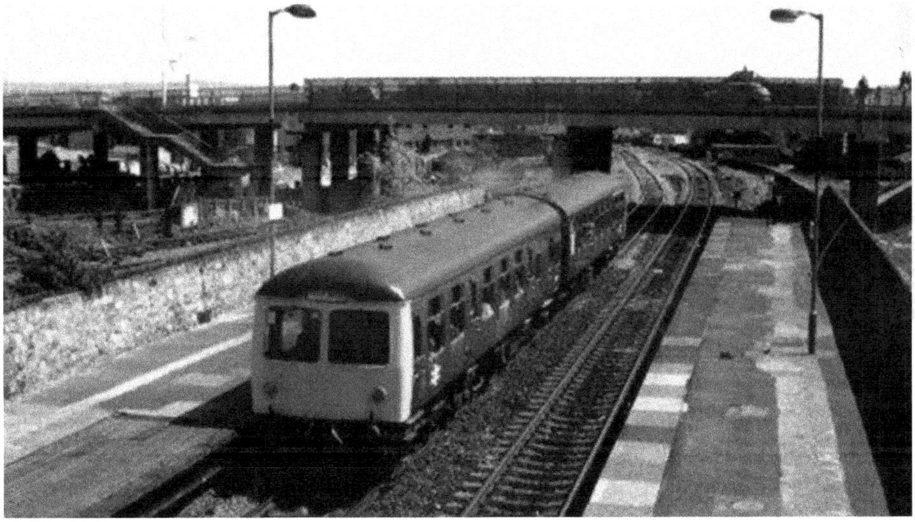

Railway Station

The former railway station in Grant Street was built in 1872 for the use of goods wagons and foot passengers. Prior to this time, a scaled down goods-only terminal operated from a site in Wylam Street. The draughty old building in Grant Street survived and served the town on the LNER line from Newcastle to South Shields for close to a century. By the late 1960s, the building was considered unfit for purpose, subsequently demolished and replaced with two simple structures on the twin platformed station, remaining this way until the area was totally transformed for the arrival of the metro system in 1982.

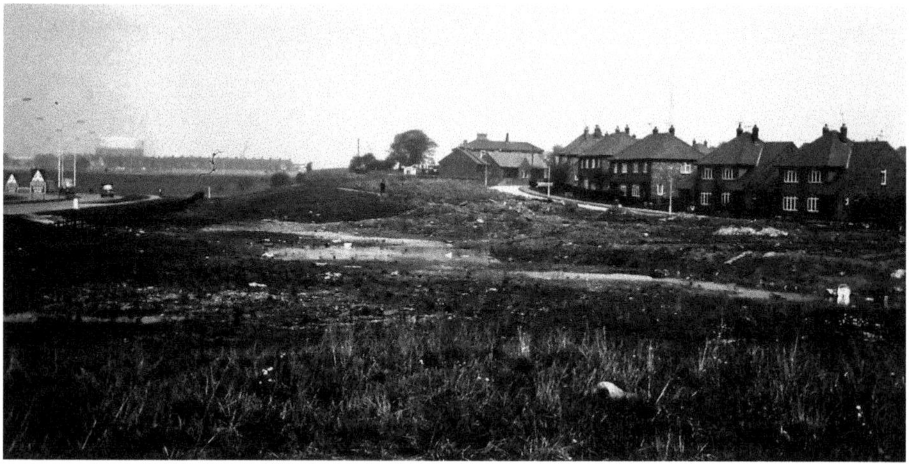

Housing at Low Simonside

Council housing was once regarded as a right for every British citizen. At the end of the First World War, the government embarked upon a massive residential housing programme. By the outbreak of the Second World War in 1939, an excess of one million houses had been provided, including replacements for those properties damaged during the Blitz. But it was the Conservative government's reign during the 1980s that took a radical change of direction with their innovative 'right to buy' scheme. This gave the working classes the opportunity to scale the property ladder by offering them the right to buy their council accommodation.

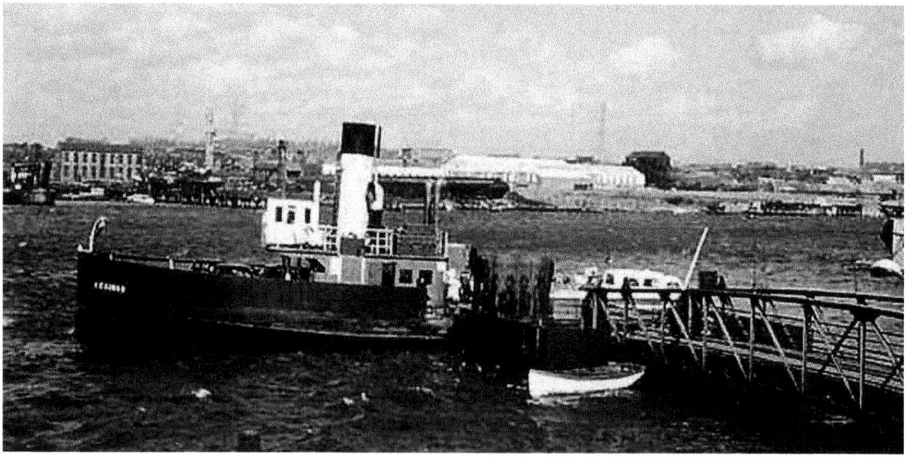

Ferry Service

For centuries people have been crossing the Tyne at Jarrow by any means available to them, until a recognised horse and passenger ferry was introduced in 1883. Built by Palmers, the *Dexter* saw service, along with sister vessel *C M Palmer*, until they were withdrawn from service in 1923. From this time, vessels *A B Gowan* I & II were introduced, providing a service for motor vehicles until the inauguration of the road tunnel in 1967. During the 1980s, the area was extensively modernised with the introduction of a public pier and walkway.

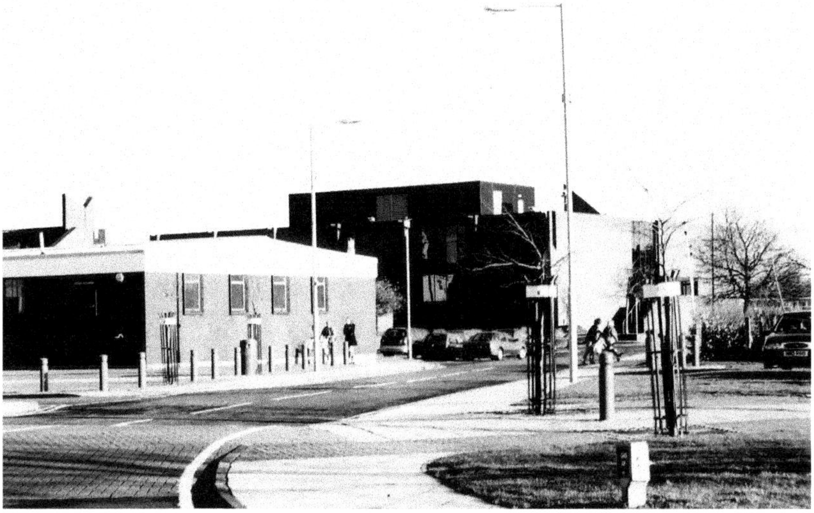

Public Lending Library

The town's first public library was situated in a disused grain warehouse in Ormonde Street, until a purpose-built unit was erected on Bede Burn Road during the 1950s. By the 1970s, the tiny building was thought to be unfit for purpose. A more convenient location on derelict land at Cambrian Street became available during the early 1970s and remained there until 2018, when it was relocated once again, this time to the Jarrow Focus within the community centre, where it supports a variety of public activities. Pictured: the former library at Cambrian Street.

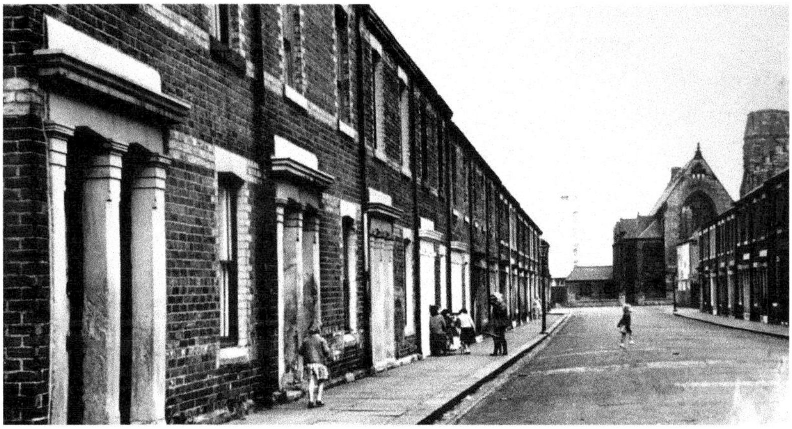

A New Beginning

The 1960s witnessed the nationwide development of 'new towns', all promising a better lifestyle with a more carefully planned tomorrow, designed to replace the ravages of war and the mass unemployment that Jarrow endured during the 1930s and 1940s. This was definitely a more positive move towards a new beginning; for Jarrow, it was the advent of the Arndale Centre in 1961. A bright and modern complex that boasted in excess of 100 shops in a traffic-free environment, the first of such shopping malls in Great Britain. Pictured: Clyde Street, 1962.

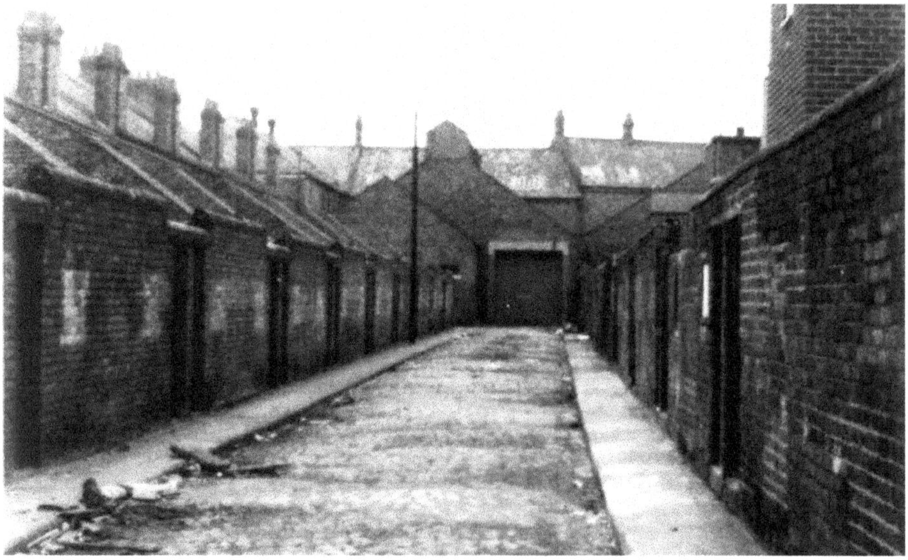

Typical Rear Lane and Yard

Above and below: Row upon row of terraced accommodation in Jarrow, which most residents were familiar with. Together with many similar-sized towns in working class, industrialised Britain, Monday mornings were usually set aside for wash day. Up until the early 1960s, women usually busied themselves doing the weekly family wash in a wash house at the bottom of the backyard. These freezing-cold and damp wash houses were eventually replaced with washeterias, or domestic washing machines for those who could afford them.

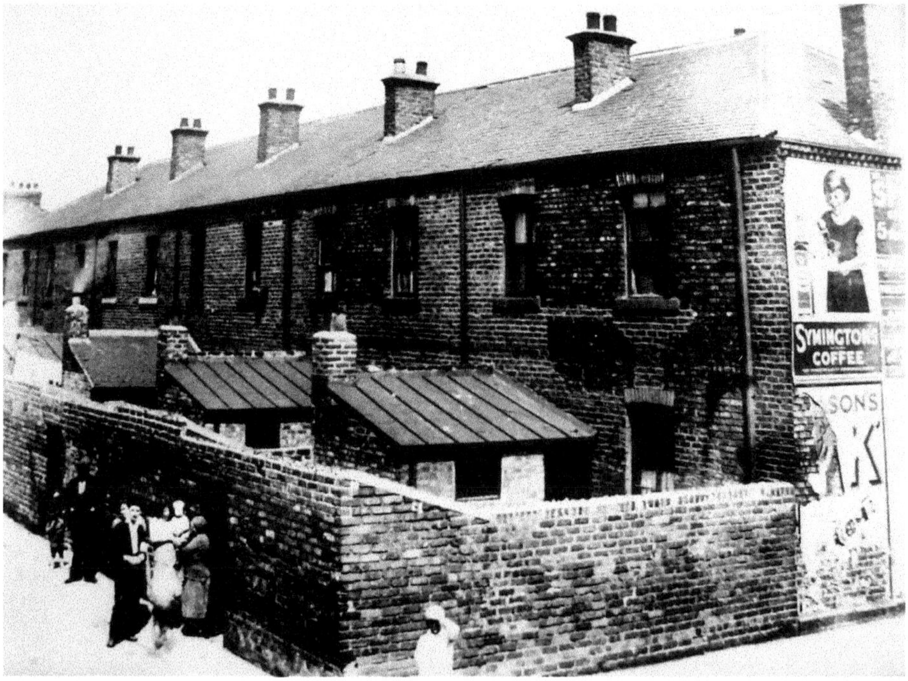

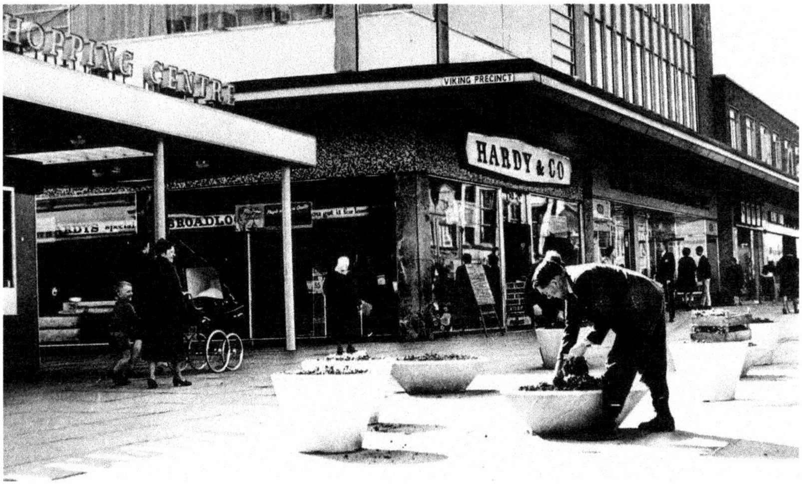

Hardy's Furniture Store

Many new businesses were attracted to Jarrow during the 'Swinging Sixties'. Hundreds of new houses were now appearing almost daily on swanky new estates. With more money in their pockets, Jarrow folk were spending freely on a variety of household goods after the abolition of wartime utility restrictions. With this free spending, the recently opened furniture shops within the precincts were supplying the majority of the modern housing with contemporary G Plan furniture. Pictured: Hardy's furniture store in Grange Road.

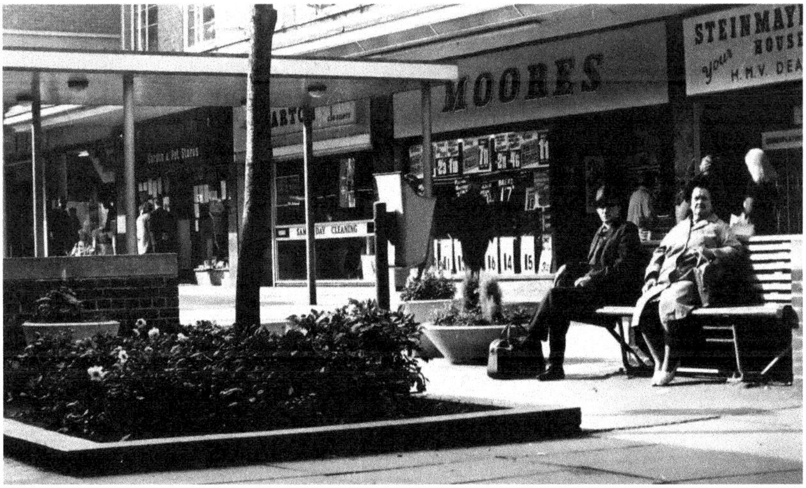

Bede Precinct

Door-to-door deliveries were made right up until the end of the 1960s. The butcher, baker and an assortment of retailers supplied the elderly and housebound up until the end of the decade, as self-service shopping began to reshape the way we purchased comestibles. The first of these such places was Moore's Supermarket in Bede Precinct, which was followed by Carlines in the arcade and, later, Presto's in Viking Precinct.

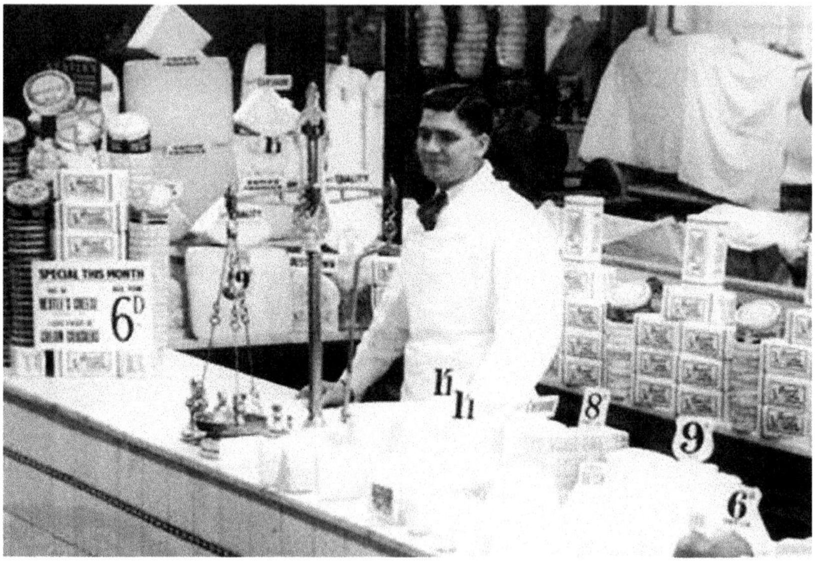

Jarrow & Hebburn Co-operative Society

As recollections of the war years and the hardship it brought with it faded, some of our towns fared better than others when they were released from food rationing during the 1950s. But it wasn't until around 1960 that shelves once again groaned under the strain of a plentiful supply of comestibles. Pictured: Jarrow & Hebburn Co-op, 1960.

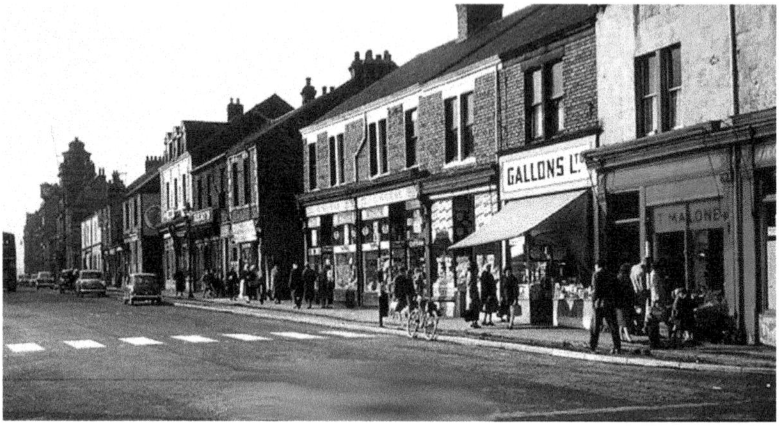

Gallons Grocery

Apart from the many corner shops within the town centre, a small proportion of grocers in Jarrow were branches of multiple organisations, similar to Hanlon's and Lipton's. But there were several opportunities for the independent grocer to earn a living vending fresh produce well into the 1960s. One of Amos Hinton's ninety-two branches traded in Western Road for several years; others, namely Gallon's, Hadrian and Duncan's, all traded in various locations in Jarrow and eventually merged during the 1970s, creating Allied Foods Ltd. Pictured: Gallon's grocery store in Grange Road.

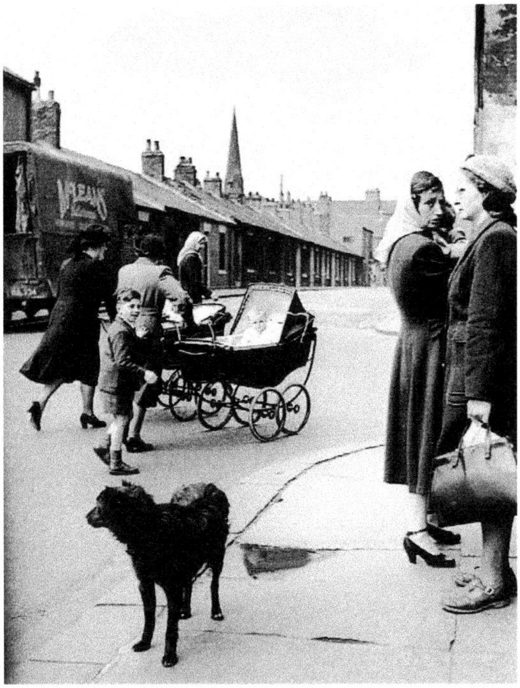

South Street

There were many shops in Jarrow dealing in second-hand furniture during the tighter years. Second-hand dealer John McLean relocated his business from Grange Road to the former Burton Tailoring building in Ormonde Street during the mid-1960s. From this time, the company specialised in vending modern new furniture, carpets and household goods, as the town became more affluent and financially secure. Pictured: McLean's furniture van in South Street.

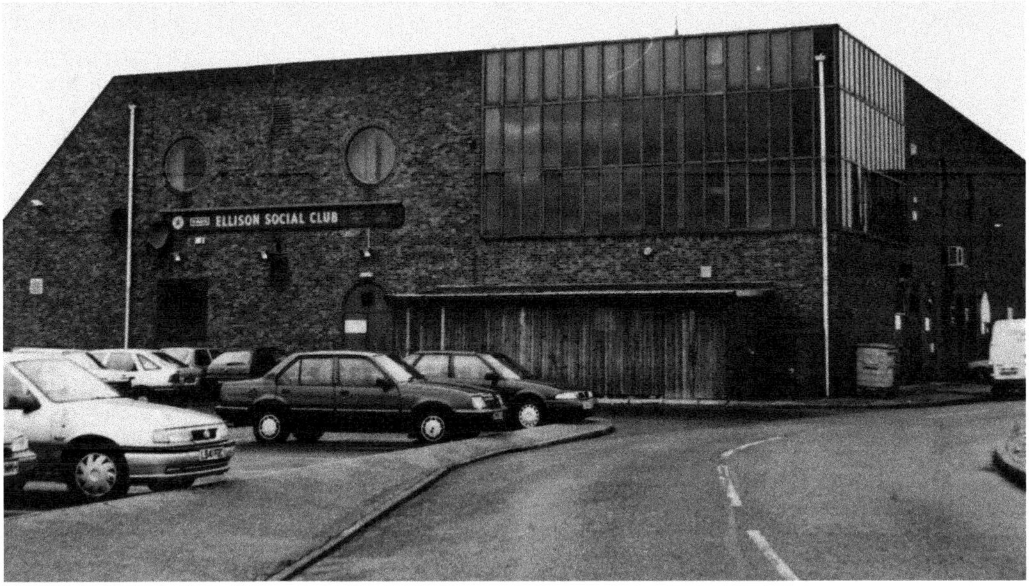

Ellison Social Club

The Ellison Social Club was located in Ellison Street. The Buffs Club, as it was more commonly known, was the Jarrow branch of the RAOB: the Royal Antediluvian Order of Buffaloes. Formerly a house more than eighty years ago, the fascia was altered in 1961 to meet contractor's criteria by conforming to the style of buildings in the immediate vicinity, and it remained this way until the premises was vacated in 1984 in favour of a purpose-built social club, 150 metres from the original.

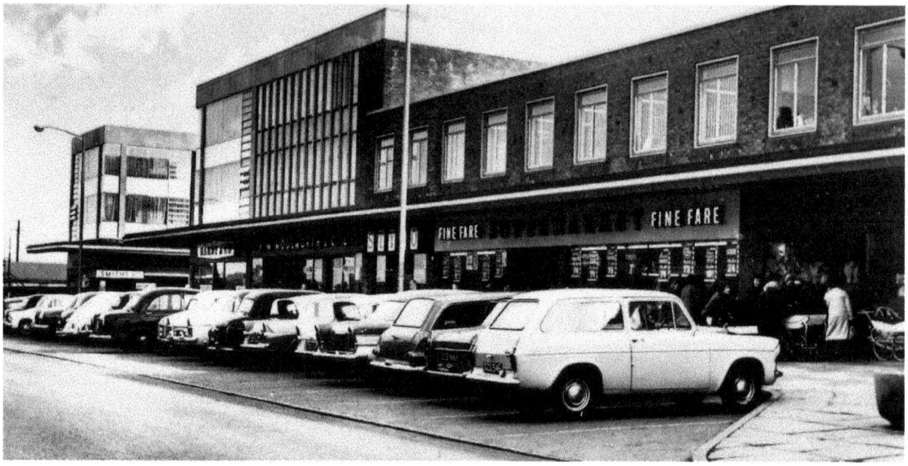

London & Newcastle Tea Company

L&N Stores in Bede Burn Road, with another branch in Ormonde Street, was the trading name of the London & Newcastle Tea Company Ltd, who purchased the Home & Colonial chain of stores soon after the end of the Second World War. Both companies served the town well until the merger. From 1961, L&N traded from a premises in Grange Road, changing their name to Fine Fare later in the decade.

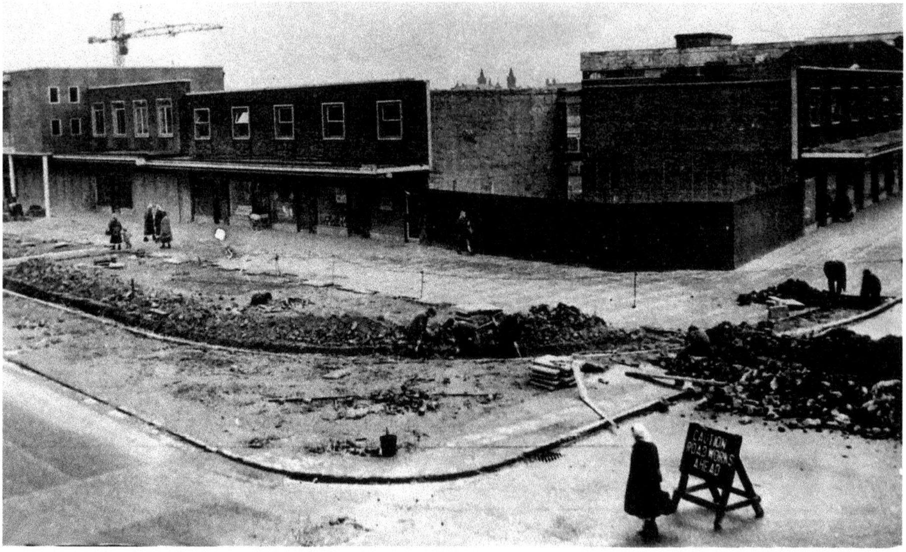

Grange Road Junction

As the Arndale Centre steadily rose from the ground, Jarrow Corporation predicted an increase of vehicular traffic and pedestrians. As the contractors provided parking spaces for an excess of 200 vehicles to accommodate this influx of traffic, alterations became necessary at some of the town's busiest junctions. This photograph from 1960, showing the alteration to the junction of Grange Road and Ellison Street, precisely illustrates the extent of the excavation.

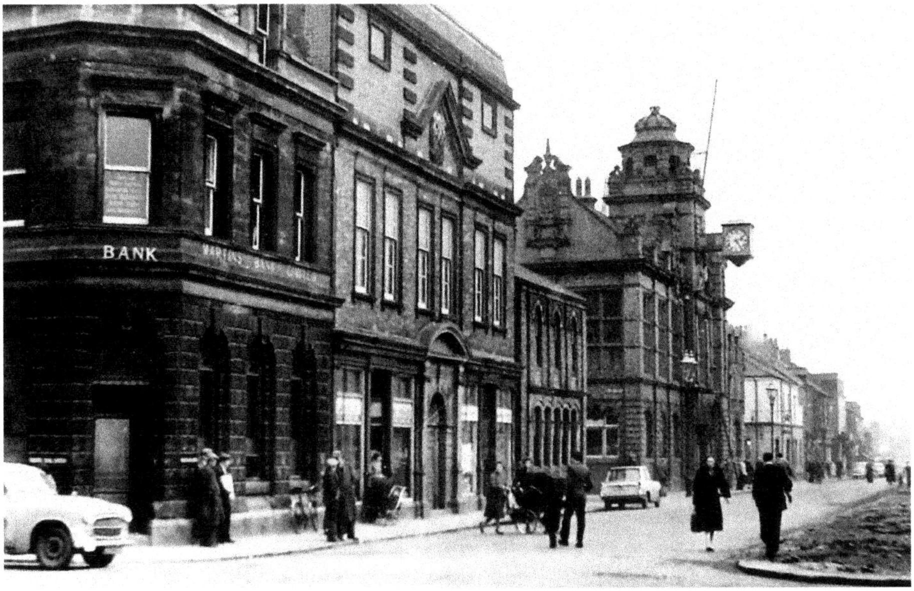

Smokeless Zone

Above and below: Because of the town's industrial heritage, Jarrow was the first town in the country to be a smokeless zone. After many years of heavy engineering, and of course the prosperity that went with it, some of the town's finest buildings became blackened with sooty deposits. Concerns about long term health issues prompted 'operation clean up' during the 1970s, when the majority of the buildings in central Jarrow were freed from this industrial grime. Pictured: Grange Road in the 1960s, and 'operation clean up' under way, 1970.

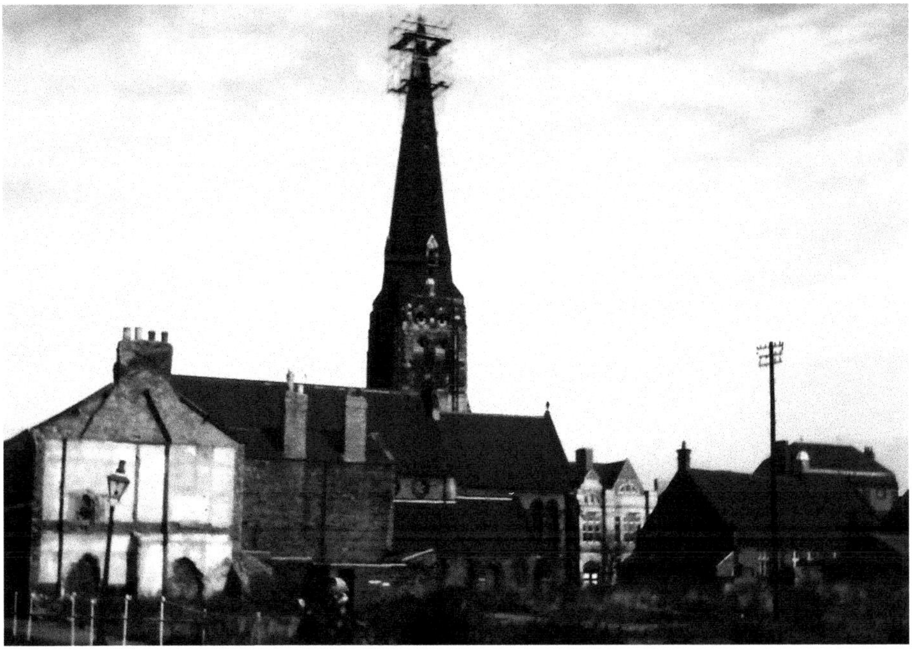

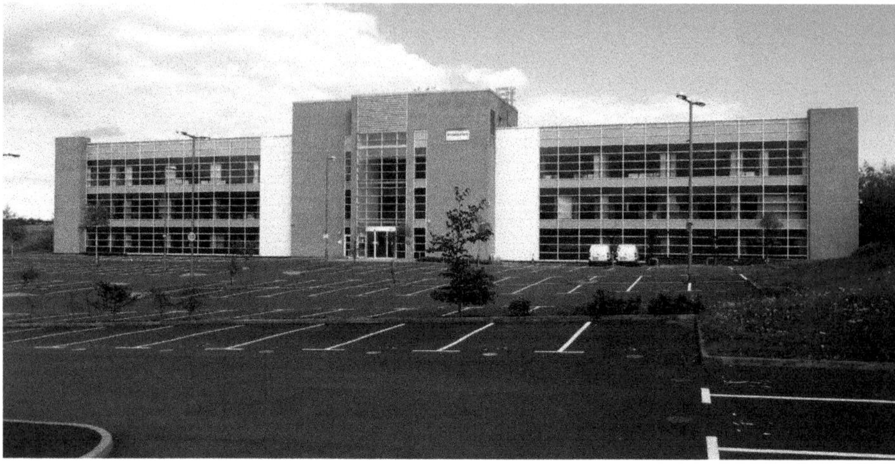

Viking Business Park

None of the industrial giants who once flourished in this part of the town survived. The land upon which they occupied has been reclaimed and replaced with an assortment of smaller factories and warehouses on the Viking Business Park, a modern industrial estate, which was formerly occupied by the mighty Palmer Empire. One of the principal occupants to the site is the Northumbria Police International Diving and Marine School, and the sub offices of South Tyneside Council.

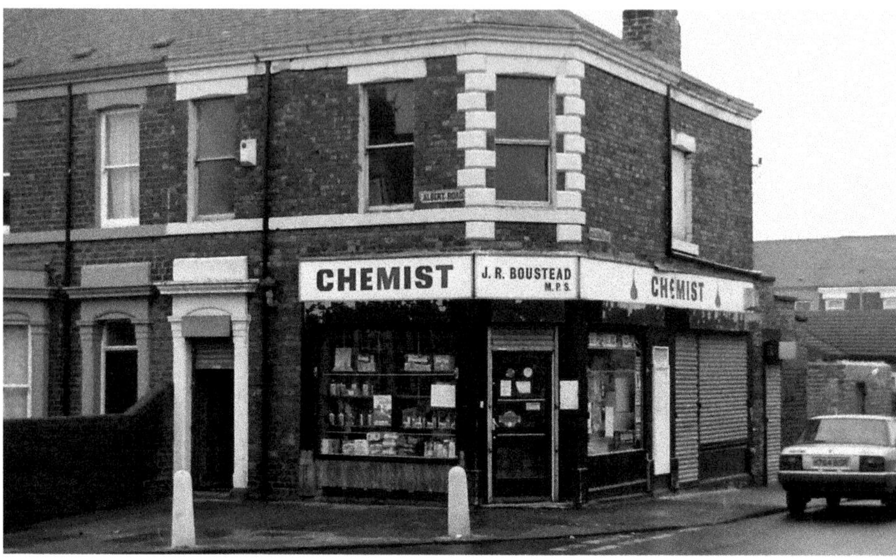

Carrick's Corner

Much of the town's realignment by the council came about during the early years of the 1970s. One major upheaval was the relocation of the traffic signals at the junction of Albert Road and Bede Burn Road (Carrick's Corner) 200 metres west to the junction of Park Road and Albert Road. This move enabled the authorities to monitor the movement of traffic in the area, re-routing increased volumes to the recently appointed Humbert Street flyover. Pictured: Carrick's Corner, 1988.

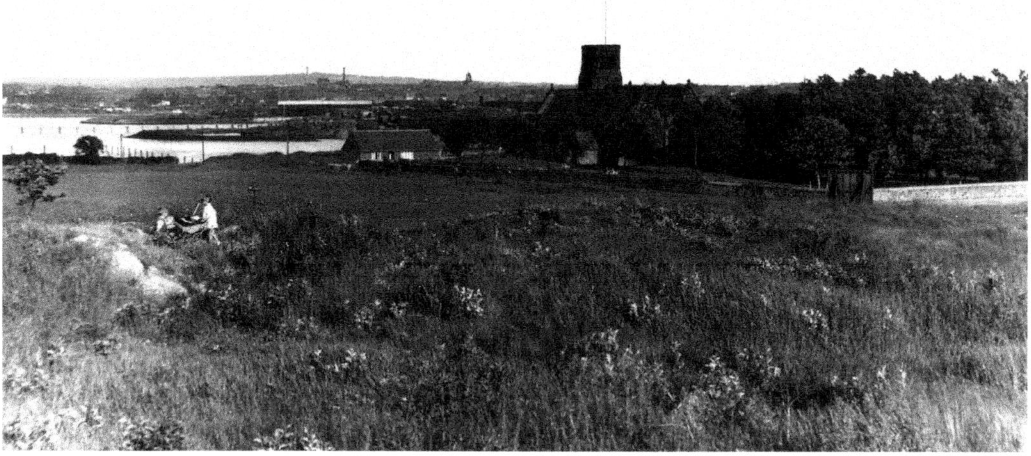

East Jarrow

For several years, East Jarrow was synonymous with prolific novelist Catherine Cookson, as this is the area she was born and raised as Katie McMullen. While distanced from the main body of the town, the area was equally self-sufficient with various industries, shops, an assortment of comfortable terraced accommodation, and more-than-adequate employment for what was a moderate population. Much of this part of Jarrow was demolished by the 1960s and the land given over to industry.

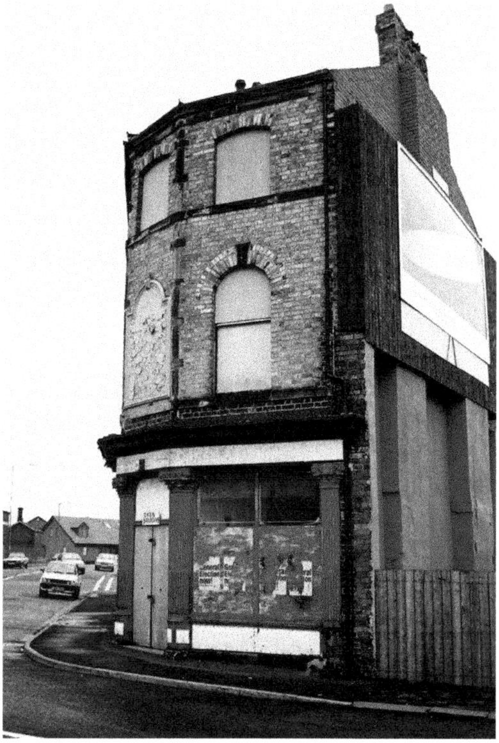

Wear Street

After fulfilling his National Service commitment, qualified gentlemen's hairdresser Joe Chatt opened a barber shop in Market Square. After a period of close to twenty-five years, the site in Market Square upon which his shop stood became subject to compulsory purchase. From this time – around 1963 – he relocated to Wear Street until his retirement in 1981, when the property was reclaimed for demolition. Pictured: The former barber shop during demolition in the 1980s.

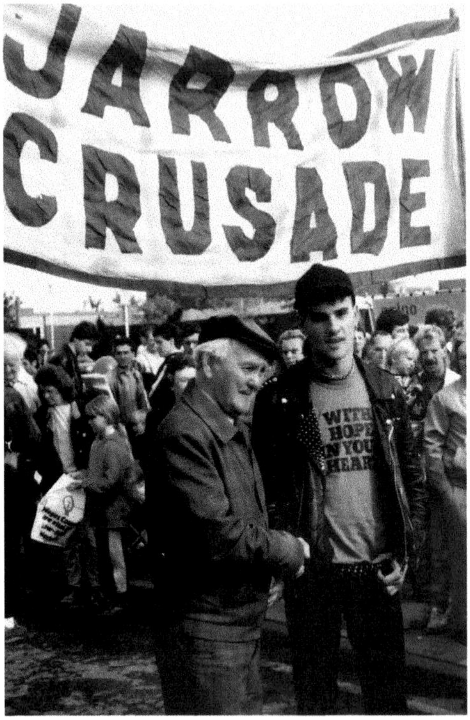

Unemployment

By 1983, with Margaret Thatcher in her second term of office as Prime Minister, conditions in Jarrow were deteriorating rapidly, and the national figures for unemployment were racing towards 3 million. In 1984, the National Miners' Strike had a devastating effect upon the people of Jarrow and the surrounding area. The government cut public spending and raised the interest rate in a desperate attempt to bring inflation under control. Pictured: Crusade to London in 1986, in protest of the unemployment situation in Jarrow.

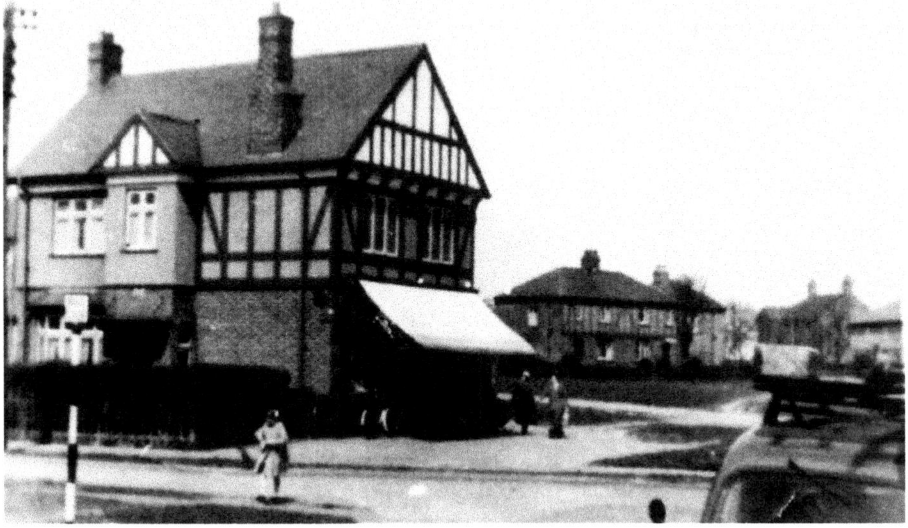

Self-service Supermarkets

After the council's mass demolition programme of the 1960s, the remaining corner shops were struggling for survival on the advent of the self-service supermarket. These self-contained stores had become the shopping destination of many housewives, and the ailing corner shops were beginning to feel the effects of their presence, who were trying every which way to lure customers away from their trusted corner shops and succeeding. Pictured: Mulholland's shop, Primrose Terrace, 1963.

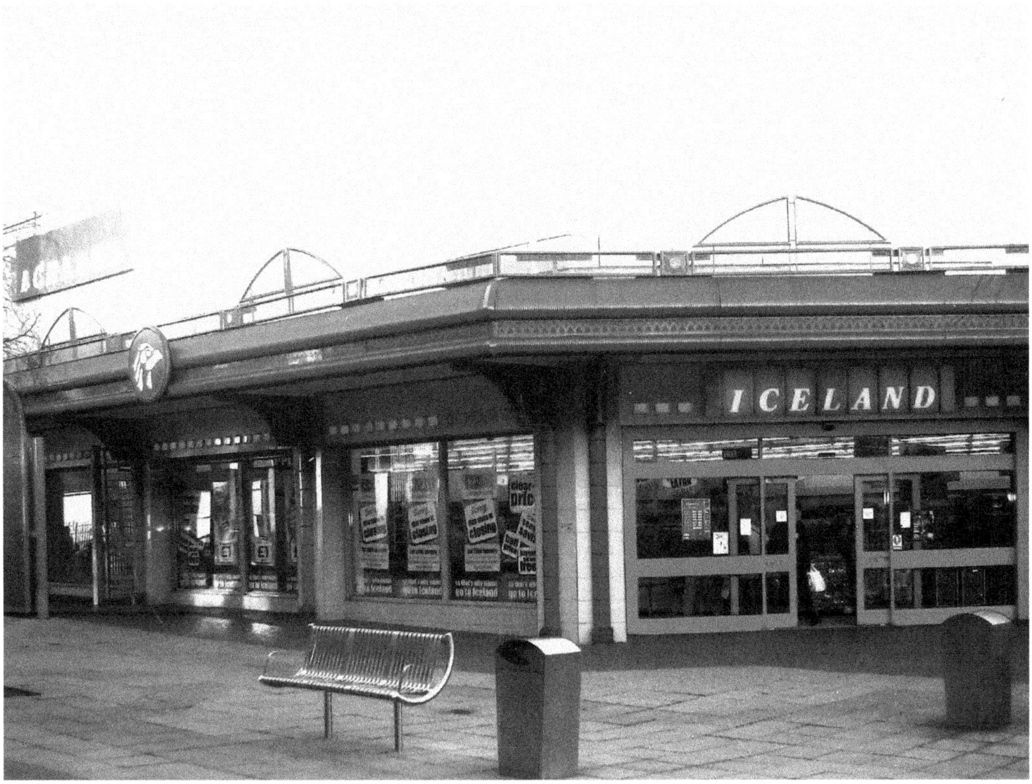

The Corner Shop

By 1979, supermarket giant Tesco had opened its fifteenth store, bringing the total to 7,000 self-service stores nationwide, while the humble corner shop was closing at a rate of thirty a week. As the war between the corner shops and rival supermarkets continued, both were now faced with a new regime of competition from freezer centres, which were set to satisfy the demand for frozen produce. This new wave of convenience store was opening everywhere, and new companies similar to Iceland, which had opened in Viking Precinct along with another close by in the Arndale Arcade, were supplying good-quality produce at very competitive prices, as domestic freezers were becoming more popular and affordable. By the middle of the 1980s, the corner shop was making a comeback right across the country by British Asian families, who were willing to work very long hours, providing up to one third of the country's convenience stores, namely under the Mace, Londis and Spar franchises right across the United Kingdom. But with many of their loyal customers now out of work, turning a profit became more difficult than ever, forcing shops to remain open even longer than before. But these measures were not without diversification, and stocking cheap plastic toys from abroad, greeting cards and magazines became necessary. Shopkeepers were now taking advantage of the many cash and carry outlets in the region, which allowed them to purchase goods at discounted and wholesale prices, cutting out the middleman by choosing and collecting goods for resale, enabling them to make a better return. This became an indispensable way for the corner shop to compete against the multiples. To achieve this goal, most of these shops were now open up to fifteen hours per day, seven days a week.

The Chairmen of the Durham and Northumberland
County Councils and of the Tyne Tunnel Joint Committee
request the pleasure of the company of

Councillor J. Flaherty

at a

Buffet Luncheon
on Thursday, 19th October, 1967
following the
Opening of the Tyne Tunnel
by
Her Majesty The Queen
accompanied by
His Royal Highness The Duke of Edinburgh

R.S.V.P.
BEFORE 30TH SEPTEMBER, 1967
TO THE CLERK,
DURHAM COUNTY COUNCIL,
COUNTY HALL, DURHAM.

CARDS OF ADMISSION WITH GUIDANCE
FOR GUESTS WILL BE FORWARDED AFTER
RECEIPT OF ACCEPTANCE.

P.T.O.

OPENING
of the
TYNE TUNNEL
by
HER MAJESTY THE QUEEN
accompanied by
HIS ROYAL HIGHNESS
THE DUKE OF EDINBURGH

Thursday 19th October 1967

Tyne Vehicular Tunnel

Above, left and opposite: The auspicious occasion of the official opening of the Tyne Vehicular Road Tunnel was presented by the Queen and the Duke of Edinburgh in the presence of civic dignitaries and tunnel officials on 19 October 1967. The Royal Train arrived at Newcastle Central Station, where they were received by the Lord Lieutenant of Northumberland. Upon their arrival at the Tunnel complex, they were invited by the Chairman of Durham County Council to view an exhibition relating to the design and construction of the tunnel. After the ceremony of unveiling a commemorative plaque, the royal couple travelled the short journey through the tunnel to the Jarrow entrance, south of the river, where they were presented to Jarrow Council Officials and Executives from Durham County Council. The mile-long tunnel was designed to reduce increasing volumes of traffic from city centres and was capable of the safe transportation of up to 25,000 vehicles daily. However, the crossing did not become fully operational until 1968. This rare invitation for Jarrow councillor James Flaherty commemorates the occasion.

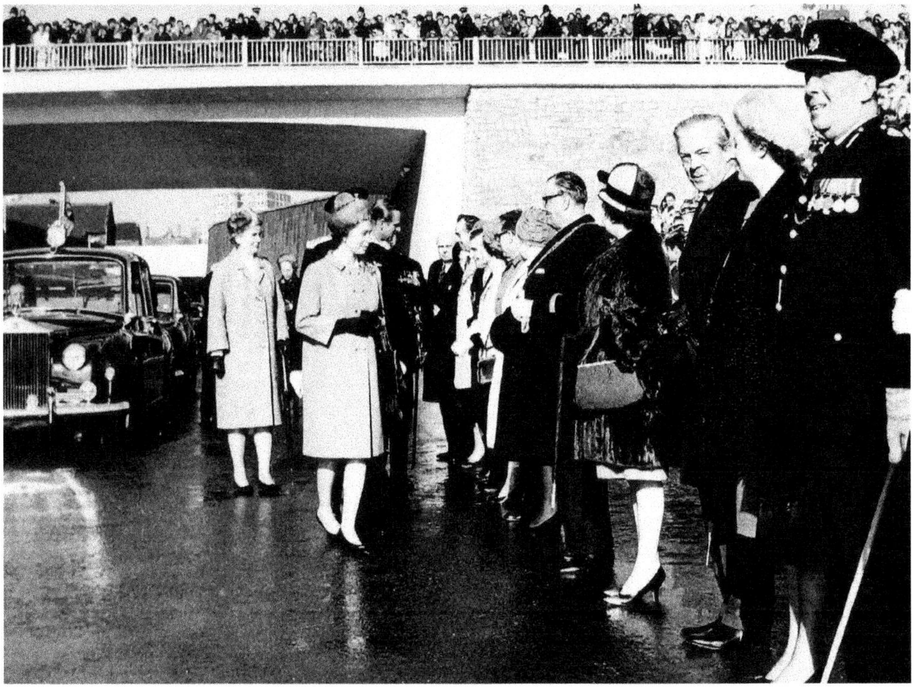

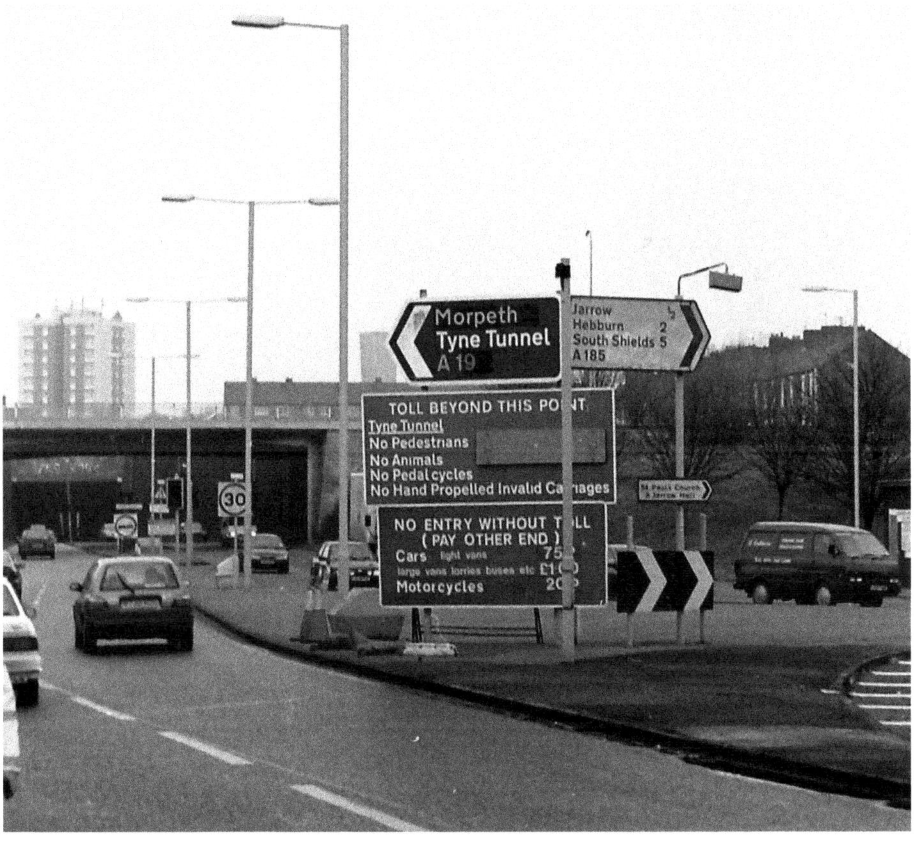
Morpeth
Tyne Tunnel
A 19
Jarrow
Hebburn 2
South Shields 5
A 185
TOLL BEYOND THIS PO NT
Tyne Tunnel
No Pedestrians
No Animals
No Pedal cycles
No Hand Propelled Invalid Ca riages
NO ENTRY WITHOUT T LL
(PAY OTHER END)
Cars light vans 75
large vans lorries buses etc £1
Motorcycles 20
30

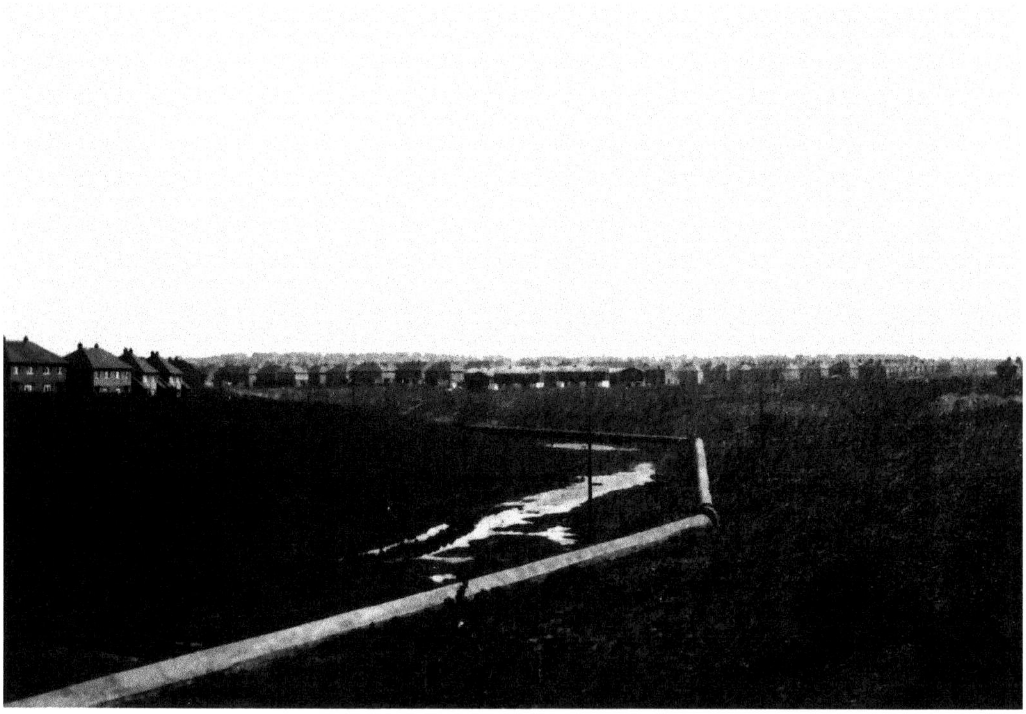

Tunnel Approach Road
As work commenced on the £8.5 million Tyne Vehicular Tunnel in 1960, a further £3.5 million was required for a network of approach roads and dual carriageways, which would eventually link the A19 south of the tunnel to the A1 in Northumberland. The construction of the southern approach road severed a valley at Low Simonside, which resulted the removal of The White Pipe, necessitating in the relocation of an alternative route for the safe disposal of the sewage it once carried. Pictured: the site currently occupied by the A19 Tyne Tunnel approach road in 1960.

TIME GENTLEMEN, PLEASE

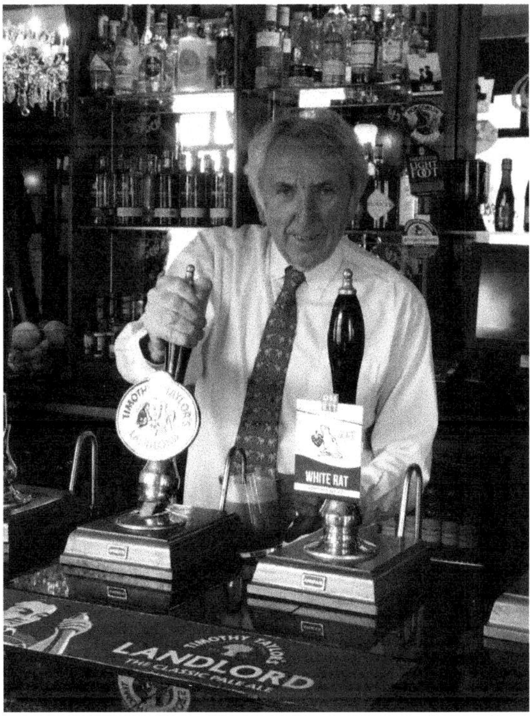

Mine Host Jess Mcconnell

Right and overleaf: During the years of the complex history of the town, one of the most memorable features of Jarrow for many was the abundance of public houses, which numbered more than fifty-four and were concentrated in and around the town centre. Many of the publicans and licensees of these watering holes were very well-respected characters, with many a tale to tell. But perhaps the most prolific and energetic entrepreneur of them all must surely be the mine host, Jess McConnell. His dream of becoming a publican was realised in 1983 with the acquisition of his first public house, the beginning of an impressive list. The Queens Hotel in Western Road was the beginning of a long and illustrious career in the hospitality industry, spanning close to four decades. After an extensive refurbishing programme later in the year, the popular venue was aptly renamed the Jarrow Lad. Jarrow, at that time, was a bustling town. The factories and steelworks were flourishing, and the town had several inns and taverns in which to quench the thirsts of the many thousands who manned them. The success of the Jarrow Lad was largely due to the free and easy talent nights and first-class entertainment by the Jarrow Lads Comedy Duo, alias Jess McConnell and Terry Joyce, who had been entertaining the north-east region since 1979. The Western Road venue continued until 1987; in 1984, a tenancy of the Robin Hood Inn at Primrose Hill was agreed with a three-year lease. This was followed in 1987 with the Victoria Park Entertainment Complex in the former Hebburn Labour Club in Campbell Park Road. This was the beginning of an eight-year period of purchasing disused or failing workingmen's clubs either side of the River Tyne, giving them a new lease of life.

The former High Pit Social Club at Cramlington became a magnet, drawing the crowds back to the once-popular venue with many famous names from the world of show business, with Ken Dodd, Norman Wisdom, Tony Christie and Jack Jones among the club's attractions. The McConnell Organisation went from strength to strength, acquiring no less than a further eight establishments. A brewing course in 2001 opened a new chapter in the enthusiastic publican's long list of attributes; this was followed in 2002 with the purchase of the Robin Hood Inn from Vaux Breweries, which had previously lay derelict for several years. One year later in 2003, the popular music-hall-style venue saw the installation of a small but comprehensive brewing facility. The Jarrow Brewery achieved several accolades, with the Robin Hood being named as CAMRA North East Pub of the Year and runner up in the Pub of the Year competition, with their popular ales beating all contestants at local and national level.

After a span of two years trading at McConnell's Gin & Ale House in Walter Street, the former prize-winning Jarrow Brewery closed due to lack of investment, owing to the financial crash of 2015. From this time the entrepreneur concentrated his efforts across the North East, doing what he loved: entertaining. After overcoming a series of family and financial difficulties, the unstoppable 'Jarra Lad' couldn't resist the challenge of reviving the fortunes of one of the town's oldest public houses, the Crown & Anchor in Chapel Road, until he took the reins once again at McConnell's Gin & Ale House and reverted the premises back to its original name, the Albion Hotel. Sadly, now just one of the five remaining such places trading in Jarrow in 2021.

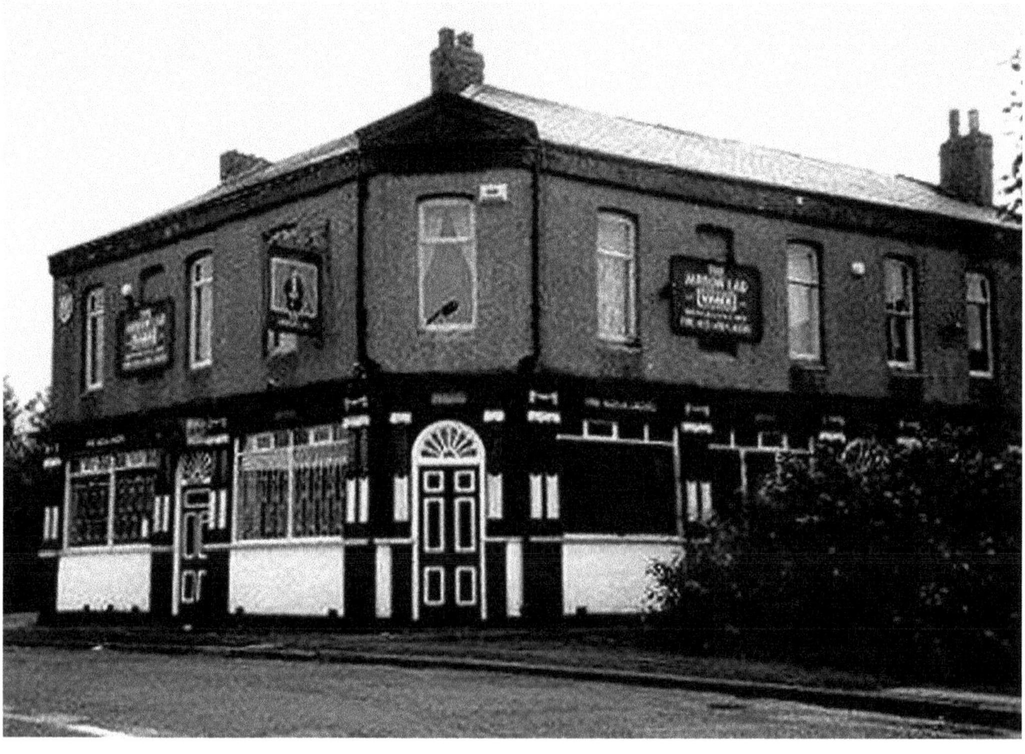

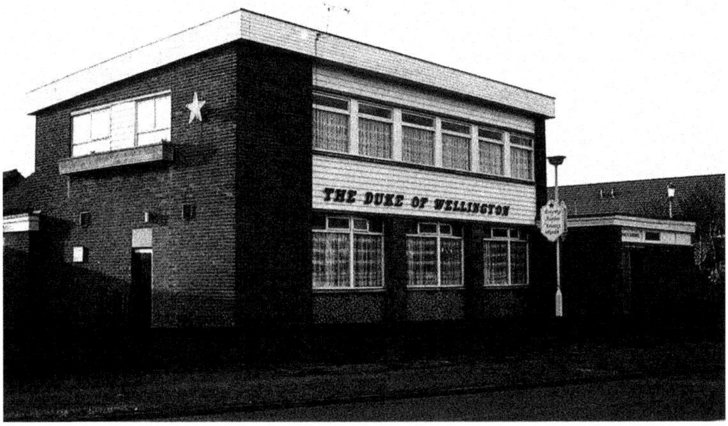

Duke of Wellington

Eating out on a regular basis had not yet reached north-east England until the 1960s. South Shields and Newcastle became the in-places for Wimpy Bars, American-style diners serving burgers, hot dogs and milkshakes. These innovative and trendy establishments attracted teenagers, especially on a wet Sunday afternoon. This form of industrialised catering spread rapidly throughout the region in a more sophisticated style during the 1970s, with the popularity of 'pub food' commencing with basket meals served at a modest price. The Ben Lomond Hotel was the first to set the trend in Jarrow, which was swiftly followed by the Cottage in North Street and the Duke of Wellington in High Street (pictured).

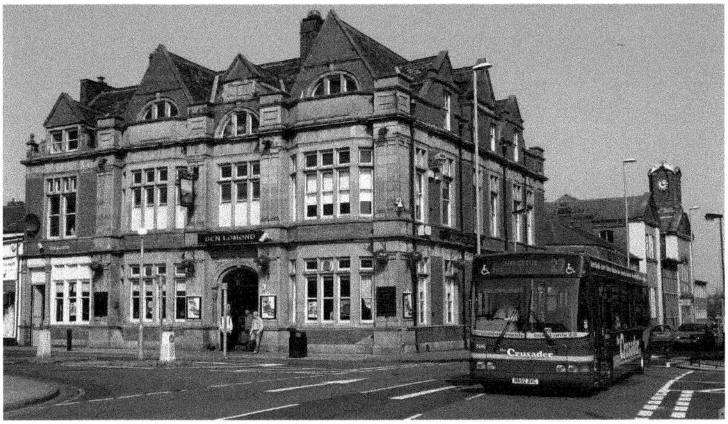

Ben Lomond Hotel

Of all the public houses within the town centre, the Ben Lomond Hotel was by far the grandest establishment of all. The Victorian building was used as a hotel and restaurant until 1970. While the exterior of the building remained much the same for decades, the interior suffered considerably through neglect. Local entrepreneur Derek Armstrong leased the building from Scottish & Newcastle Breweries Ltd, restored it to a very high standard and renamed it The Viking. By 1985, the grand old building had once again slipped into a state of disrepair, so a further restoration programme followed and the building reverted to its original name, The Ben Lomond.

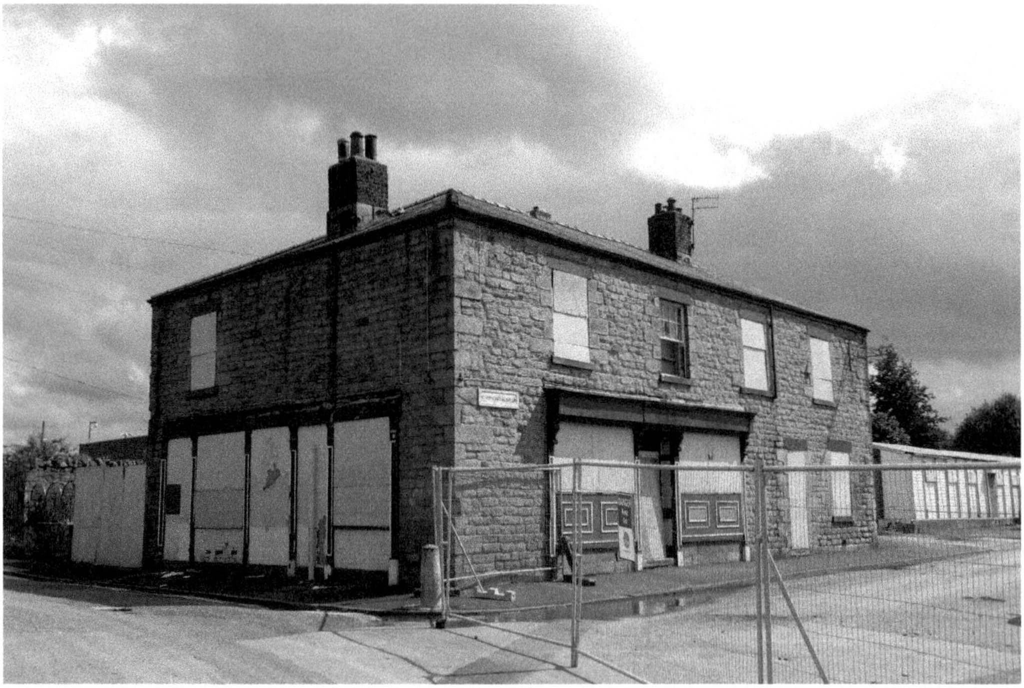

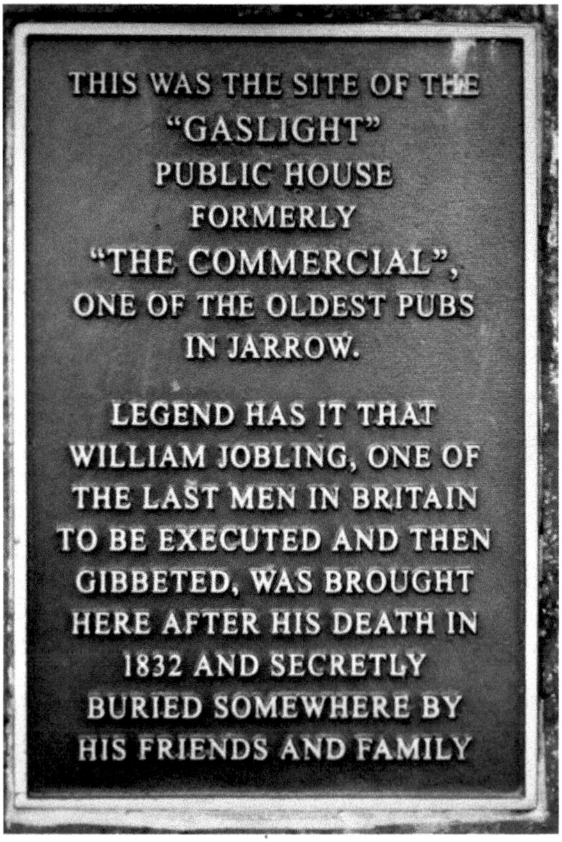

Commercial Hotel

Above and left: Formerly a seventeenth-century coaching inn, the Commercial Hotel in Commercial Road fell victim to the trend of name changing and was renamed the Tunnel Tavern during the 1970s. A further name change to the Gaslight followed soon after, until the premises were demolished, making way for further development. Today, the site displays a William Jobling memorial.

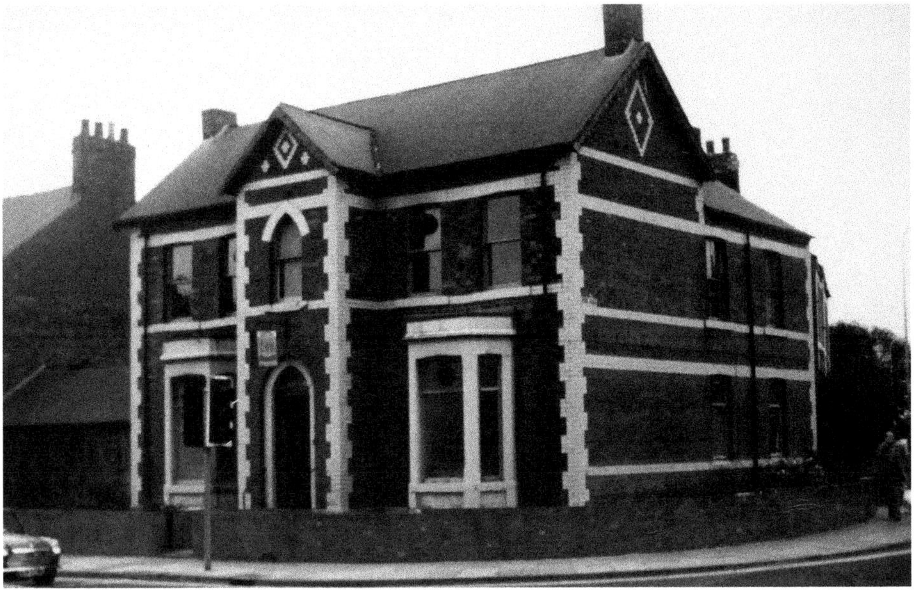

Alberta Social Club

This photograph of the old Alberta Club in Albert Road dates from 1978. Built in 1890, it was once the home of builder and former mayor of the town Zephaniah Harris, who sold it to his brother William Gladstone Harris in 1904, who resided there until 1923. By 1935, the building was refurbished and converted into a private members' club. As the popularity of the club rose, so did the need for larger premises. Building commenced in 1979 on a vacant site in Grant Street, and upon completion, the membership relocated in the early 1980s. This photograph was taken in 1975.

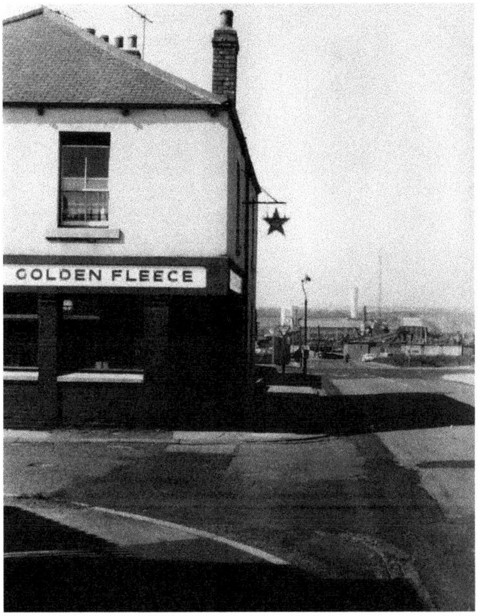

Golden Fleece Ferry Street, 1963. One of two public houses with the same name, the other being in Commercial Road.

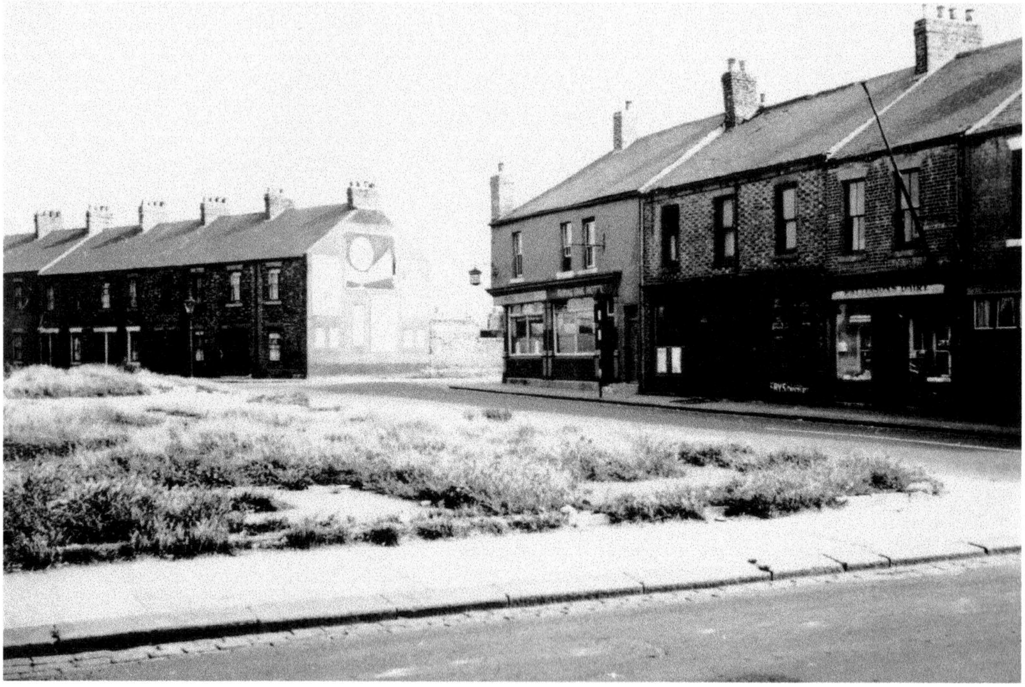

Royal Oak Hotel, Grange Road, from 1961.

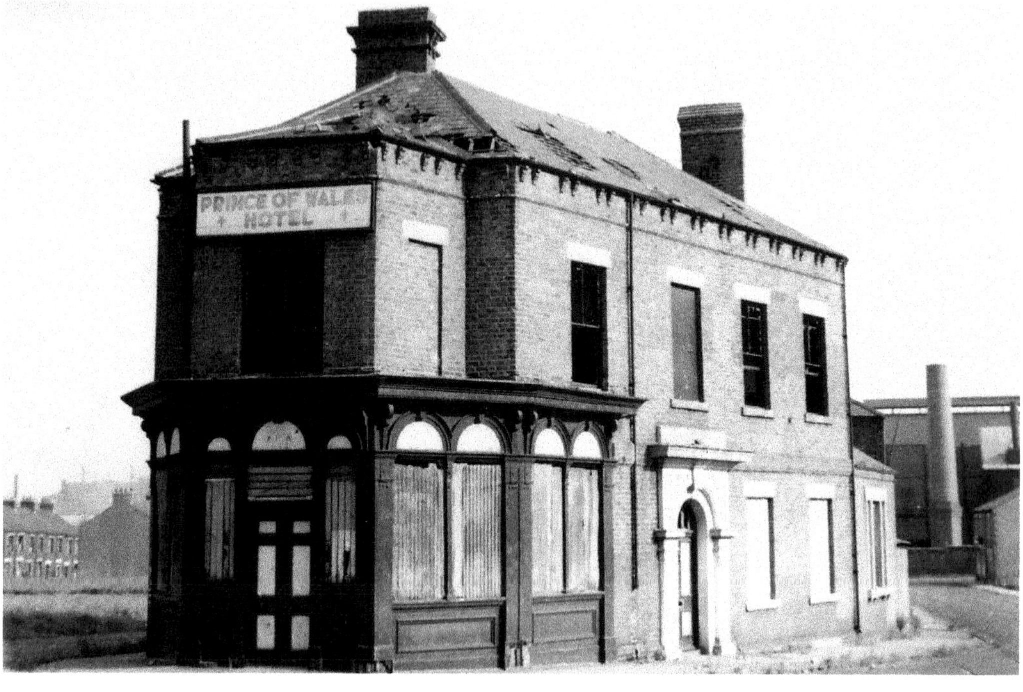

Prince of Wales Hotel, Commercial Road, 1960, relocated to a site close to York Avenue in 1962.

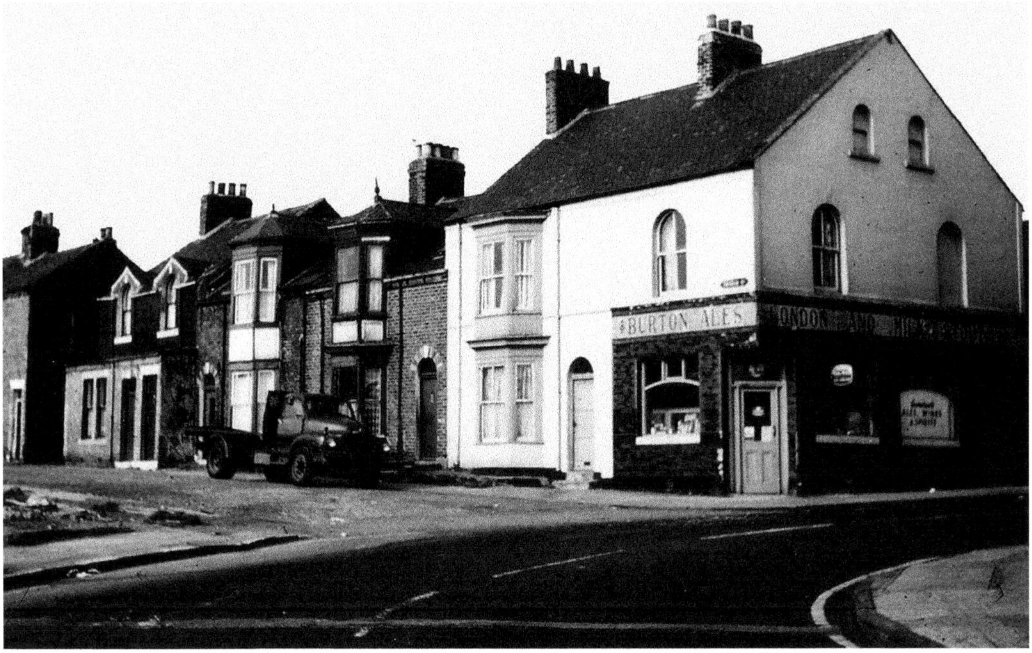

Bridge Inn was constructed for use as a public house. Local by-laws stipulated its location did not conform to the council's strict criteria and it was thus refused a licence to sell liquor. Just prior to when this photograph was taken in 1960, the premises were granted permission to operate as an off-licence.

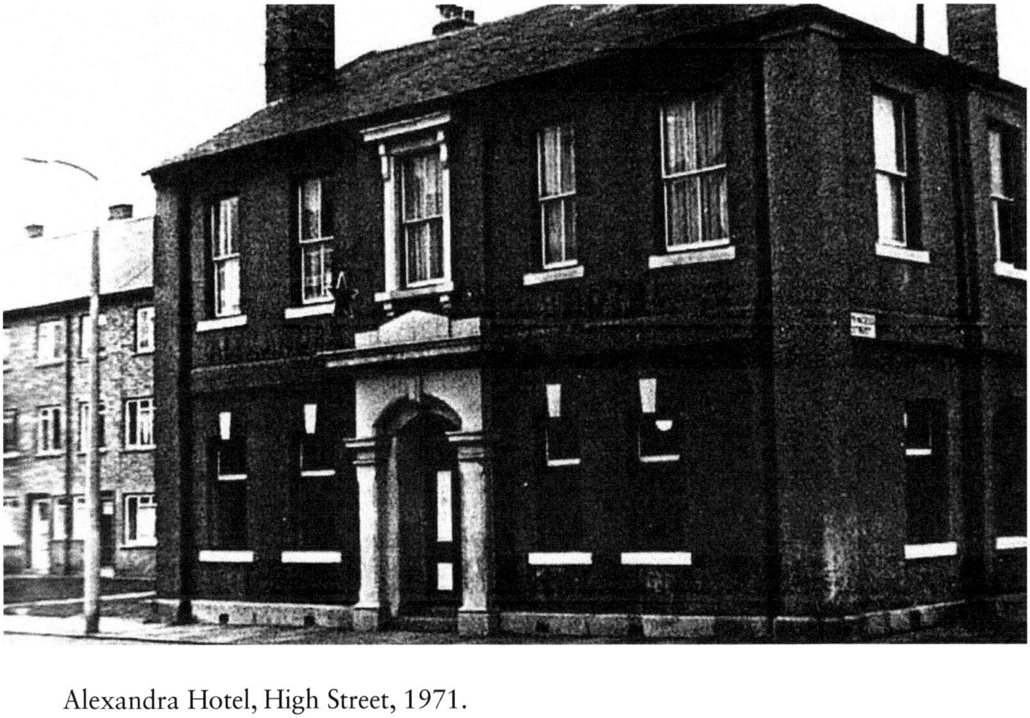

Alexandra Hotel, High Street, 1971.

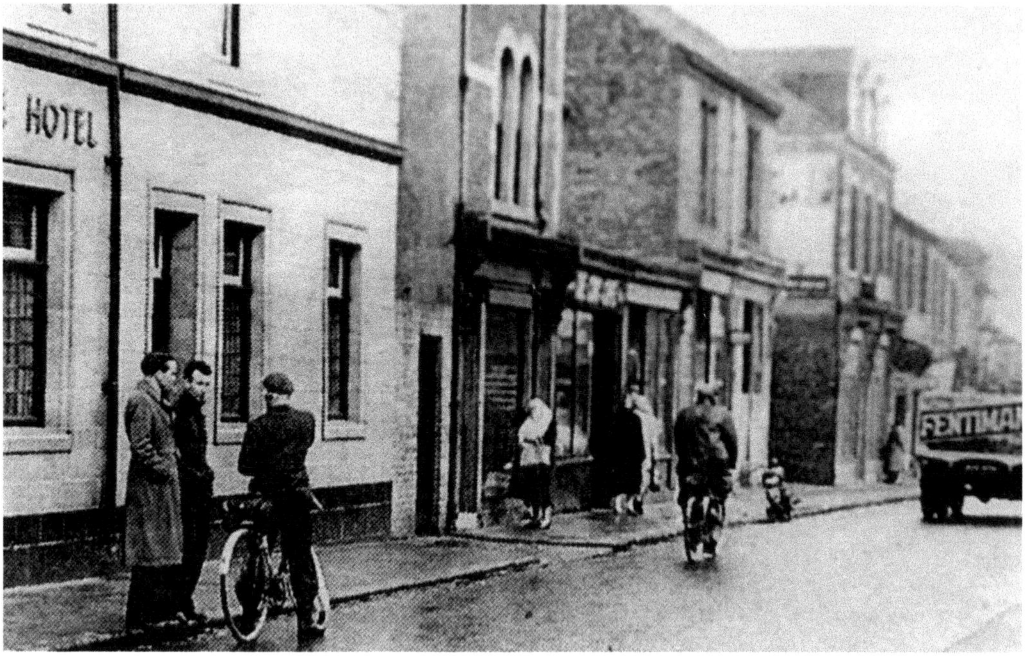

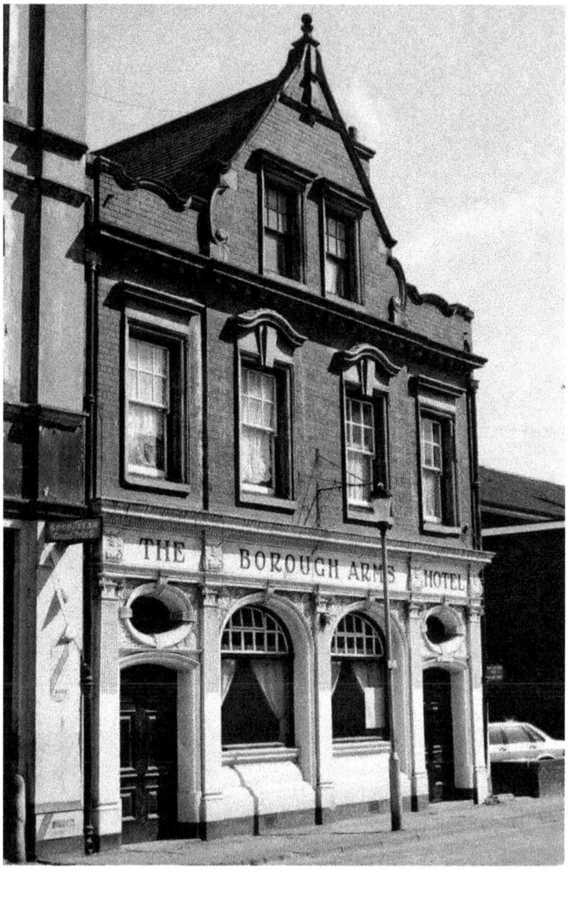

Above: Alnwick Castle Hotel, Grange Road, pictured to the left of this image from 1962, just prior to its demolition. The site is now occupied by Wilkinson Court.

Left: Borough Arms, North Street, 1979.

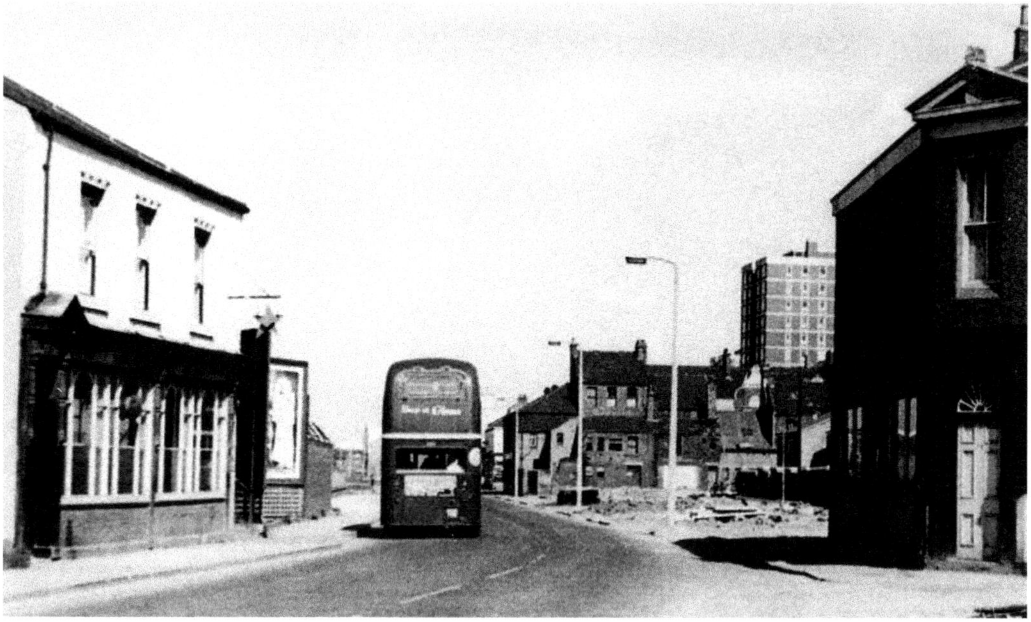

Rolling Mill, to the left of this 1970s photograph, with the Queens Hotel to the right. This became the Jarrow Lad in 1983.

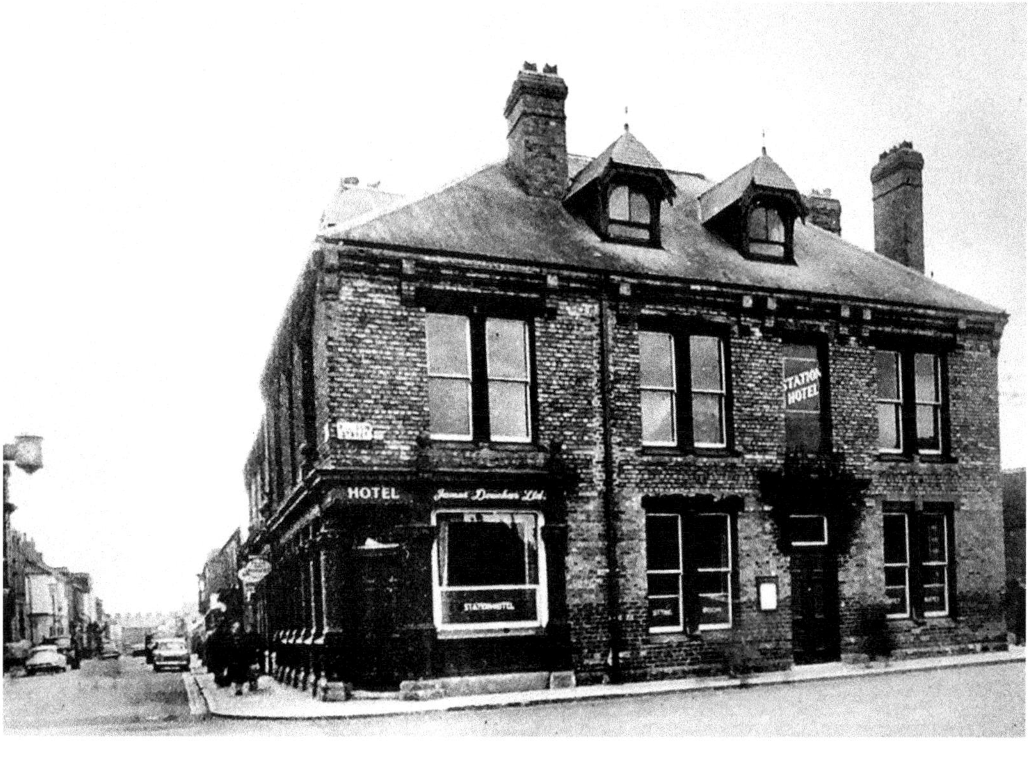

Station Hotel, Ellison Street.

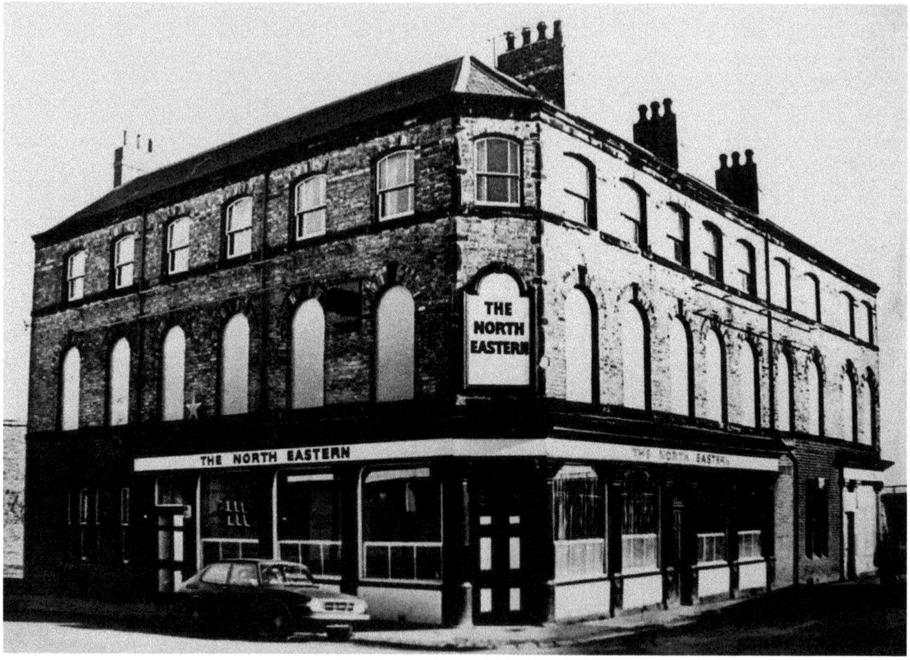

North Eastern Hotel, Station Street, was built by Charles Palmer in 1890 and demolished during the 1980s.

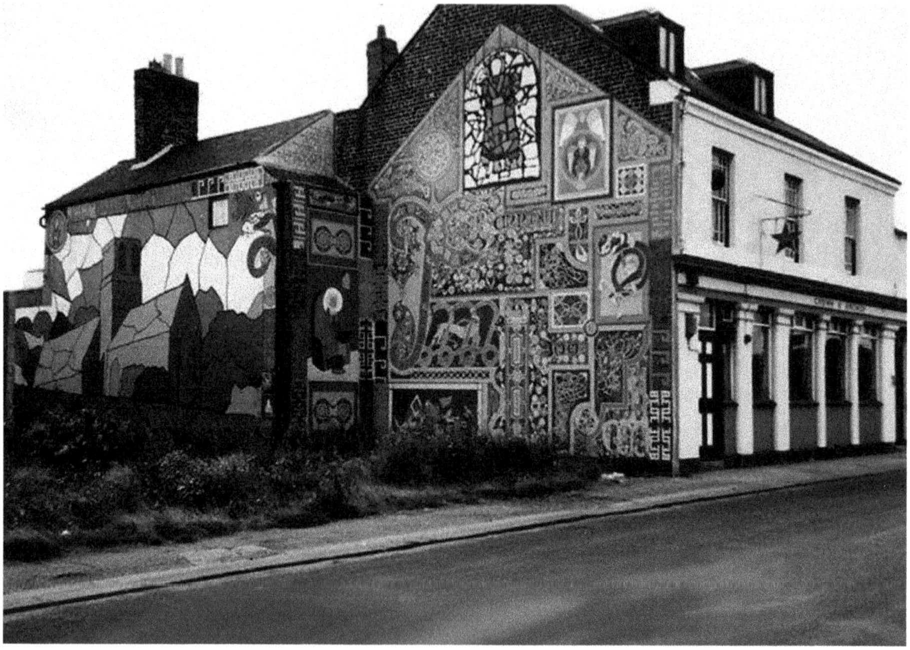

Seventies-style psychedelic art adorns this gable of the Crown & Anchor, Chapel Road.

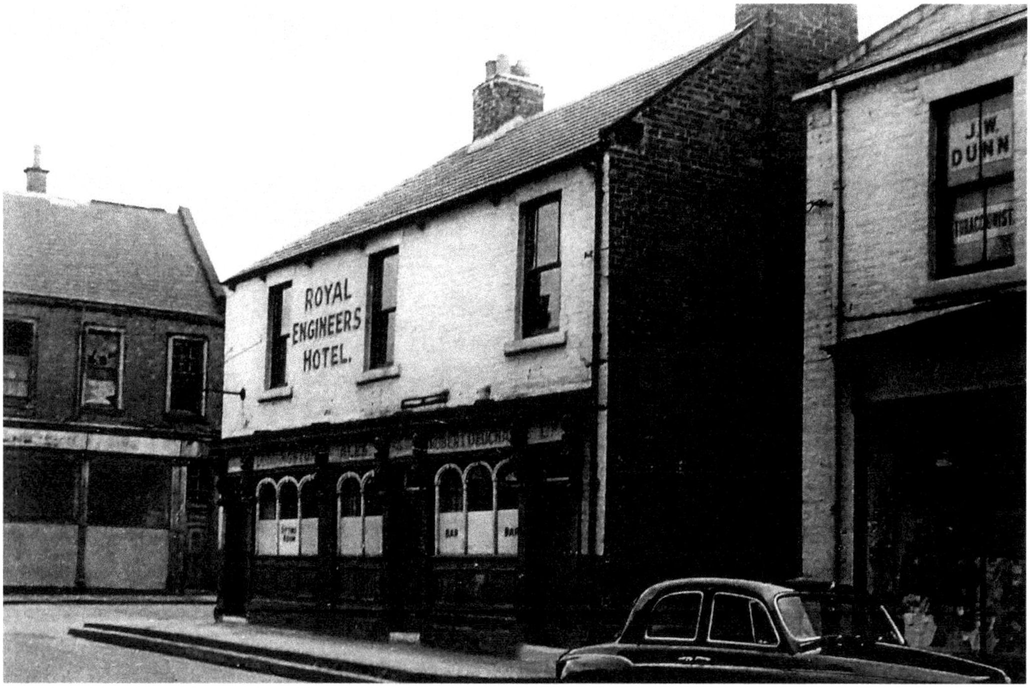

Royal Engineers Hotel, Ormonde Street, 1960.

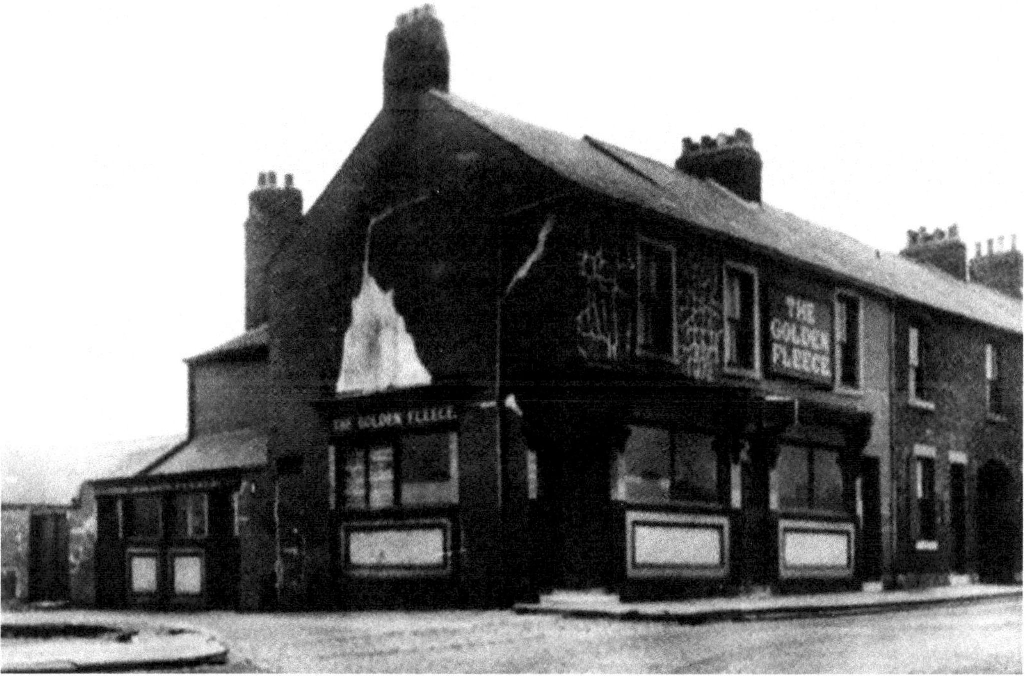

Golden Fleece, Commercial Road, 1960.

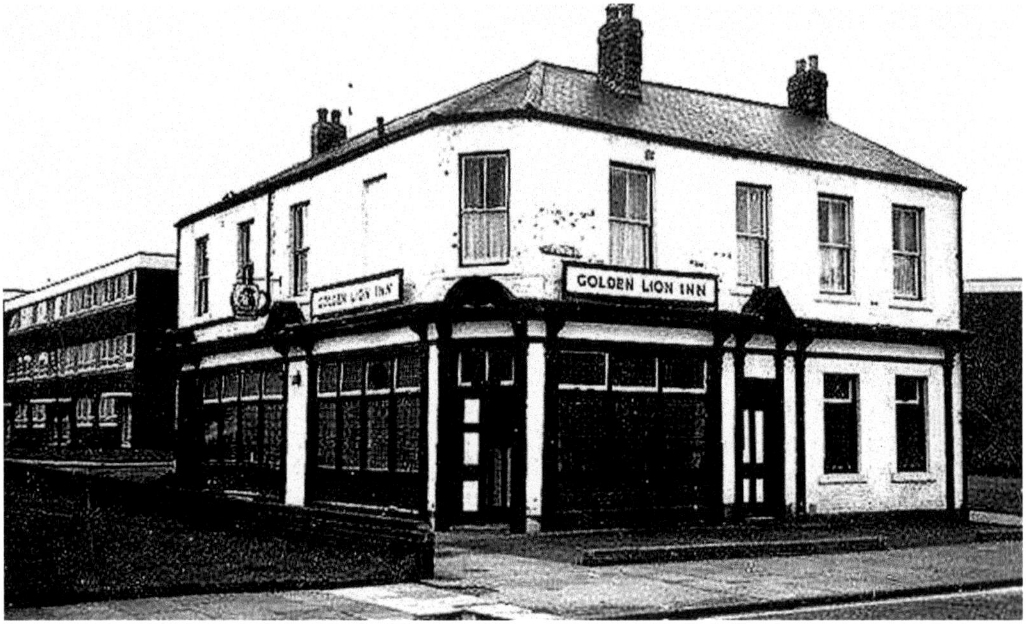

Golden Lion, Walter Street, 1983.

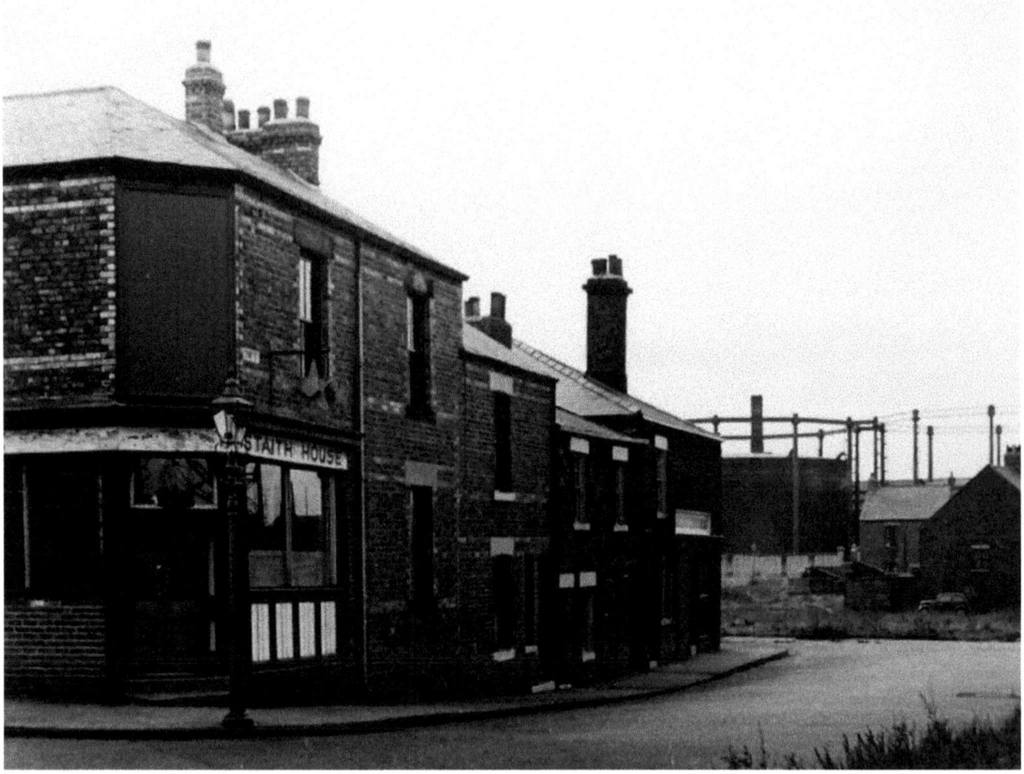

Staith House, Tyne Street, 1961.

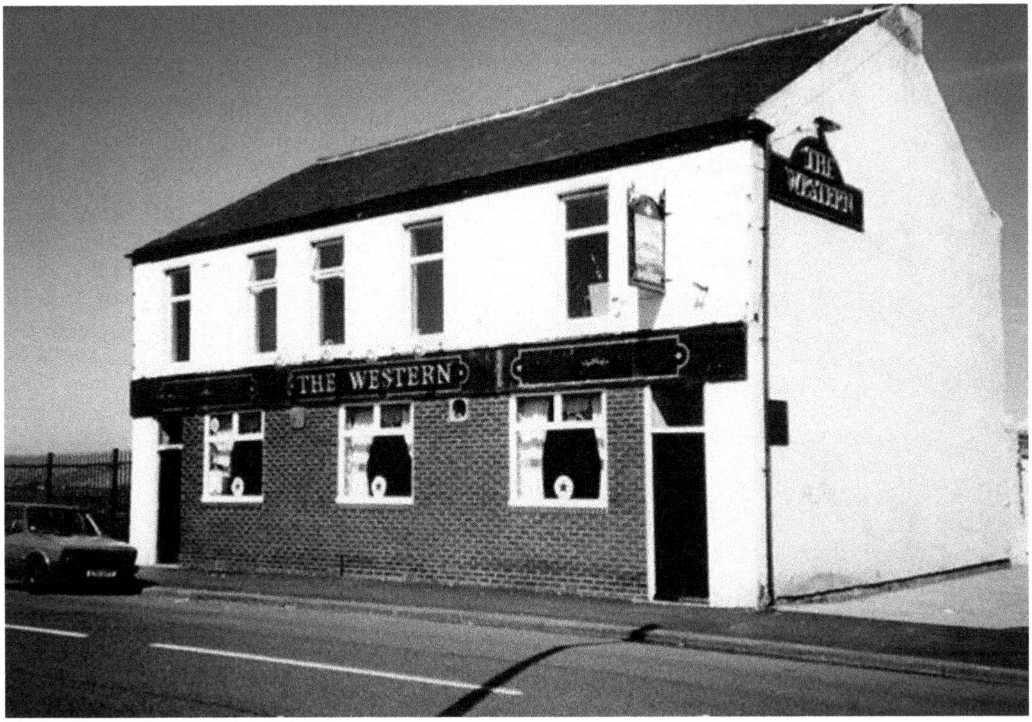

The Western, Western Road, 1976.

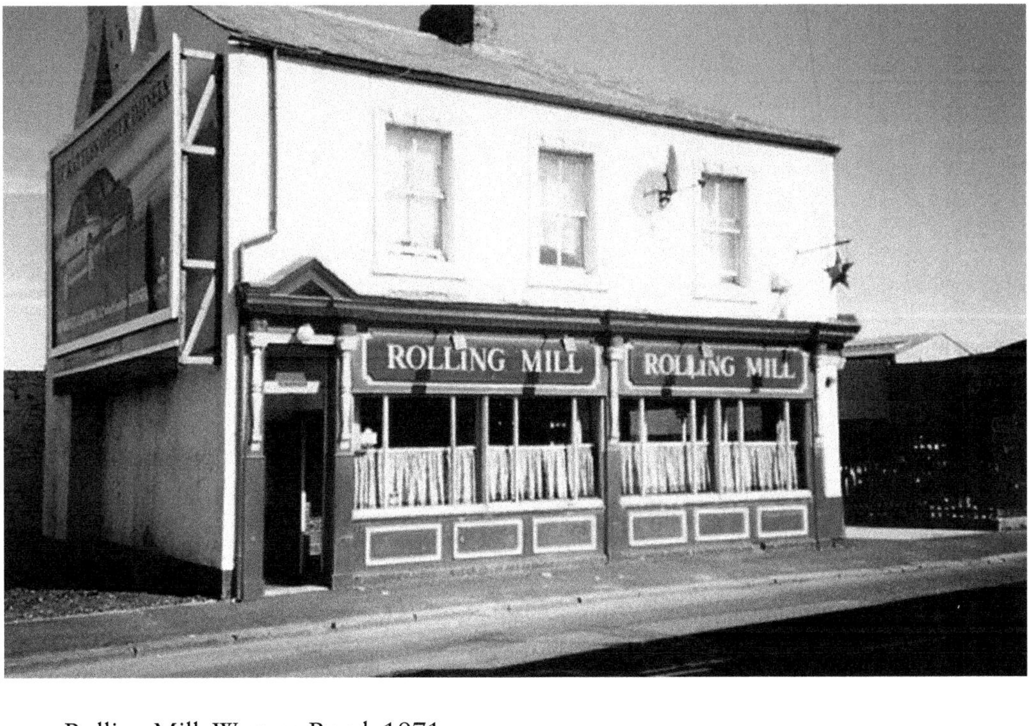

Rolling Mill, Western Road, 1971.

HIGHWAYS AND BYWAYS

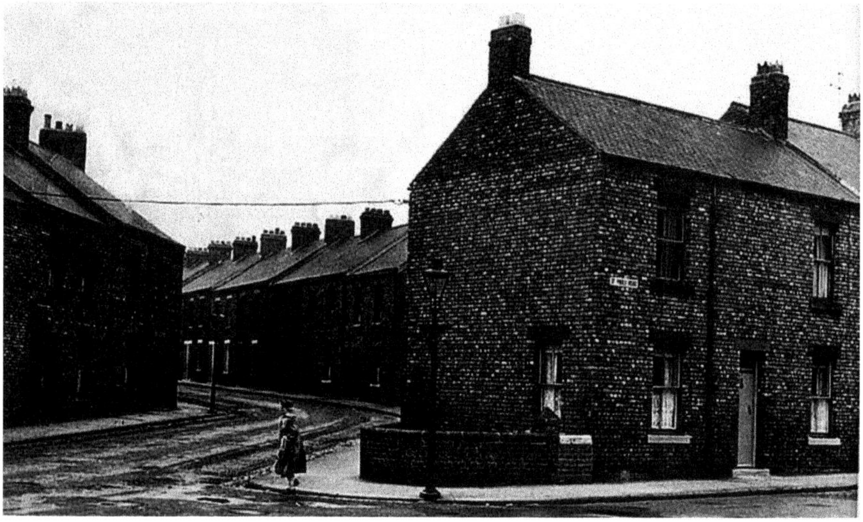

Dee Street

Above: Prior to work commencing on the original Tyne vehicular tunnel, much ground preparation work had to be undertaken, commencing as early as 1959 with the partial demolition of the accommodation in Dee Street. Construction of the crossing finally got underway in 1961, simultaneously at Jarrow and Howdon. The contractors, Edmund Nuttall & Co. Ltd, completed the excavations ahead of schedule, with the opening ceremony by the Queen taking place on 19 October 1967.

Boys' Brigade

Opposite above: The formation of the now well-established Boys' was founded in 1883 by William Alexander Smith and two brothers, James and John Hill, at a mission hall in Glasgow. As the movement grew and spread nationwide, the brigade merged with the Boys' Life Brigade in 1926. This resulted in the boy's reserve sections becoming known as The Life Boys. By 1948, the Jarrow, Hebburn and Boldon branches joined forces with the more substantial battalion at South Shields. The accompanying image of the Jarrow Life Boys is thought be from around 1960.

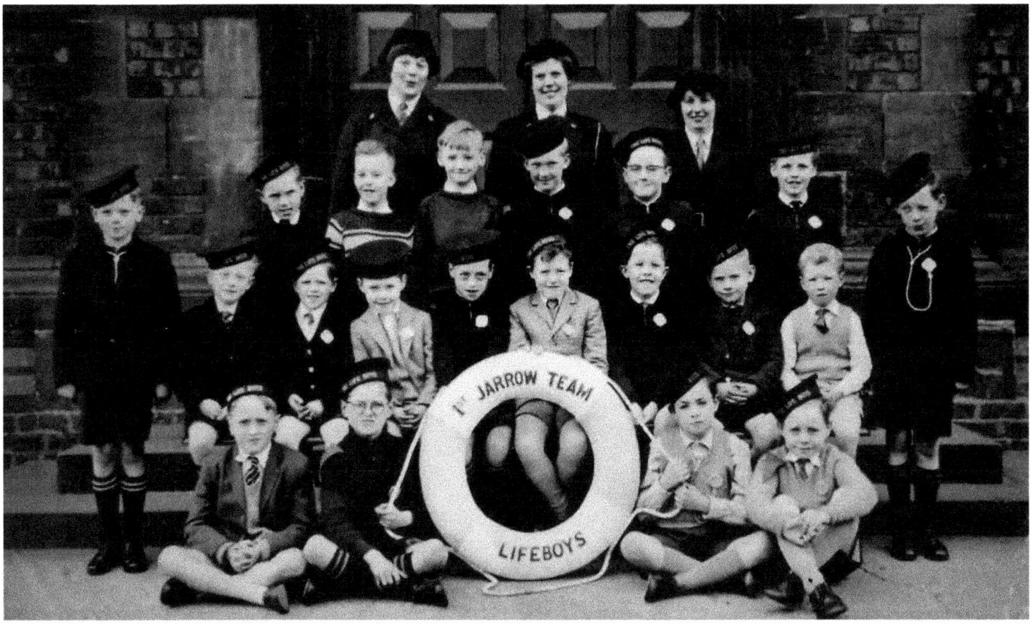

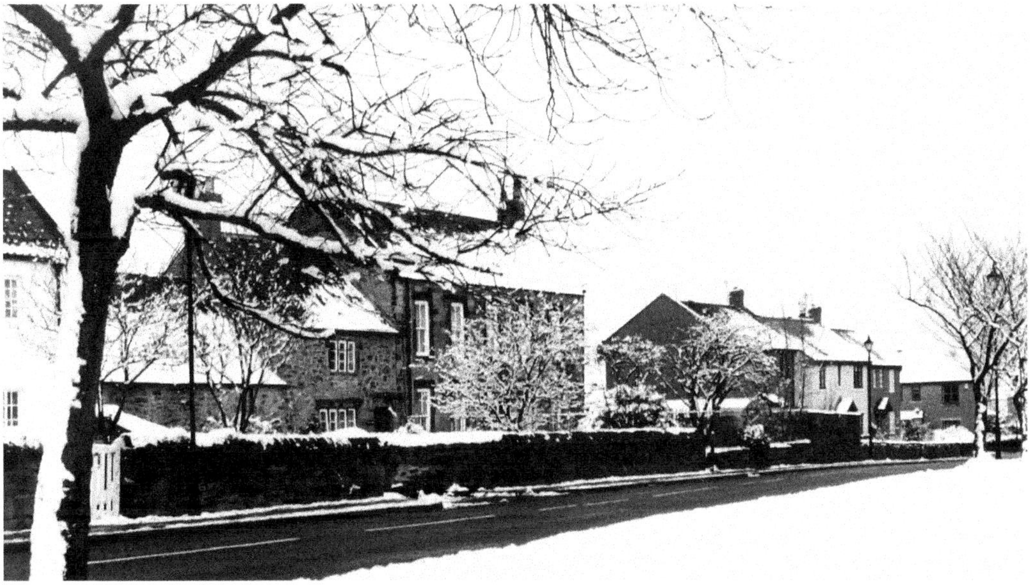

Monkton Village

The picturesque small village of Monkton has often been referred to as 'God's little acre', nestled between Jarrow & Hebburn. Tradition assigns this as the birthplace of the Venerable Bede. Bede's Well, north-east of the village to this day, retains its name and status in the history of the area. Although the spelling differs slightly to '*Be'd*' – an Anglo-Saxon word meaning 'prayer' – it gives us the name Badeswelle. Roughly translated, this means 'well of prayer'. It is believed that this little watering hole was around at the time of Bede, but it's highly probable that he wasn't aware of its existence. Contrary to popular belief, it was not the sole water supply for the monks at the seventeenth-century monastery in Jarrow.

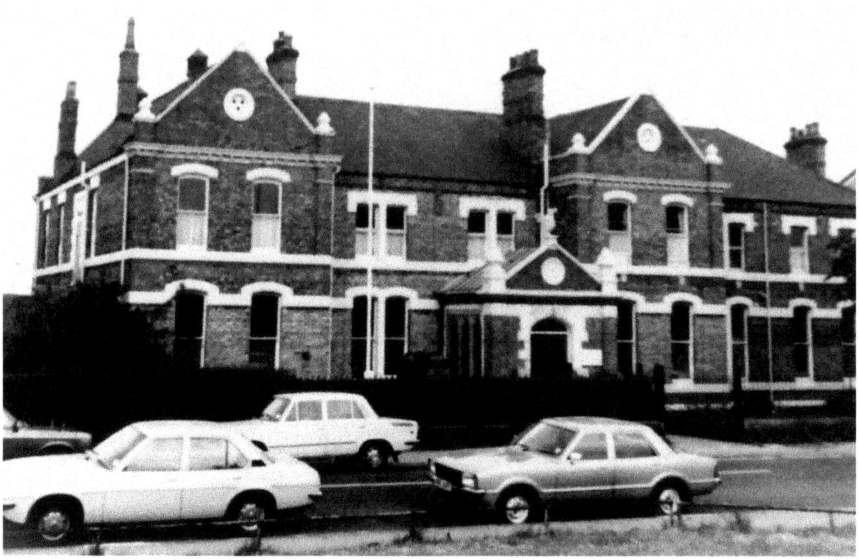

Palmer Community Hospital

Above and below: The original Palmer Memorial Hospital in Clayton Street was gifted to the town by Palmer himself, who dedicated the building to the memory of his first wife, Jane. By the 1970s, the facilities of the ageing hospital were deemed inadequate for modern medicine and subsequently demolished and replaced on a site similar to the original, but with a more modern and up-to-date establishment, which was officially opened by Princess Anne in 1984. These are two images of the hospital: firstly, the original in Clayton Street, 1972; secondly, the new building under construction in 1982.

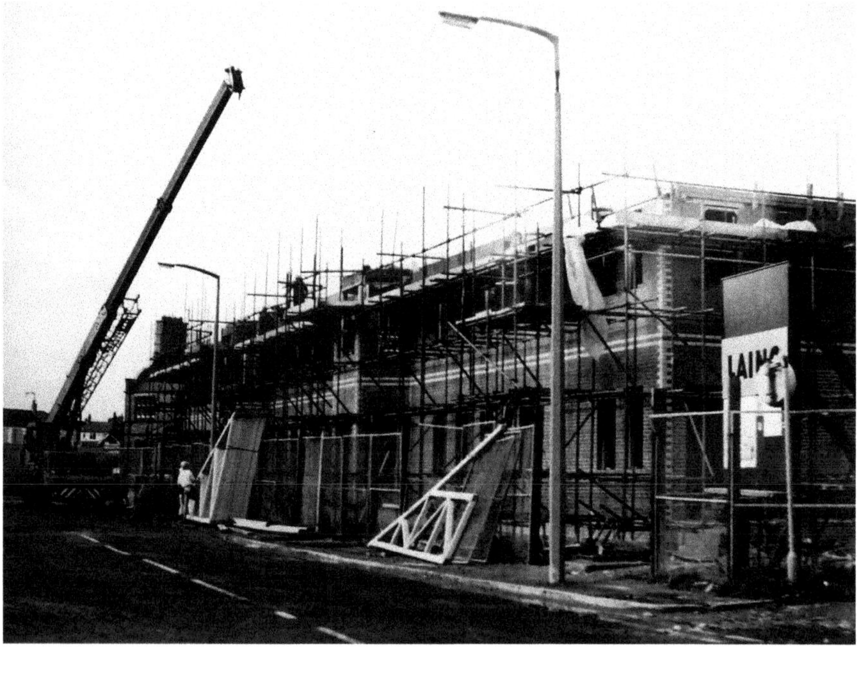

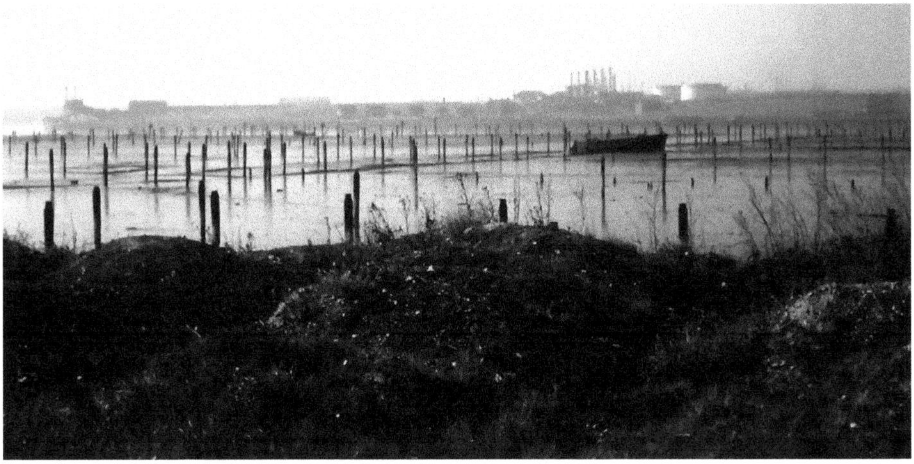

Jarrow Slake and Slake Road

Above and below: The Saxon word 'Gyrwy' has long since morphed into Jarrow. A translation reads 'marsh or fen', and it was from this translation that the town took its name. The expanse of water, known locally as the Slake, a name that it has been known by for centuries, is nothing more than a merger of Jarrow's Lake. On several separate occasions, centuries apart, Jarrow Slake was used by the Romans to anchor their vessels at the mouth of the River Don, and by King Egfrid to shelter the whole of his fleet from the savage northern winters, and again by the plundering Danes. The Slake itself was an extensive wasteland occupying an area of almost 1,000 acres, covered with water from the spring tides. In more recent times, this barren, sheltered basin was used for maturing timbers. At the 1963 annual general meeting of the South Shields based Smiths Docks Ltd, the chairman announced the company had secured and was about to purchase a substantial area of land occupied by Jarrow Slake for the purpose of the construction of pontoon blocks capable of accommodating battleships, steamers and eventually cruise liners. However, after giving the project further consideration, the company decided against further investment and development. The accompanying images date from 1972.

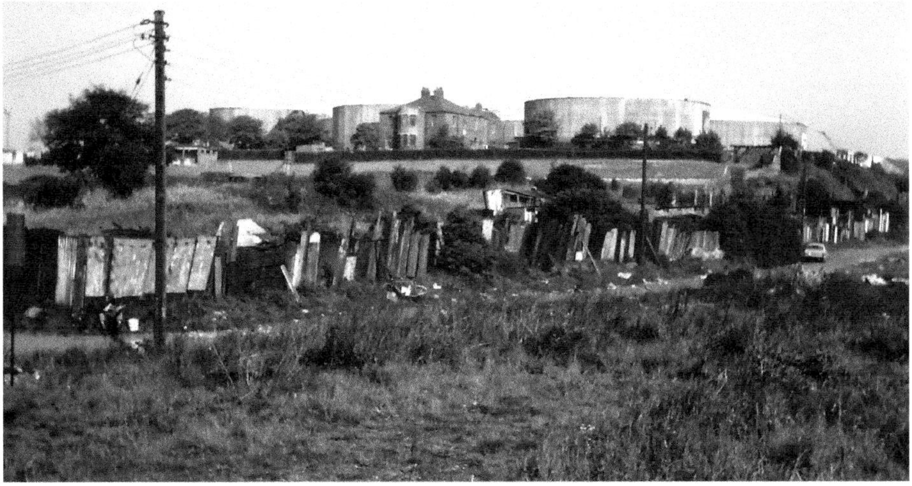

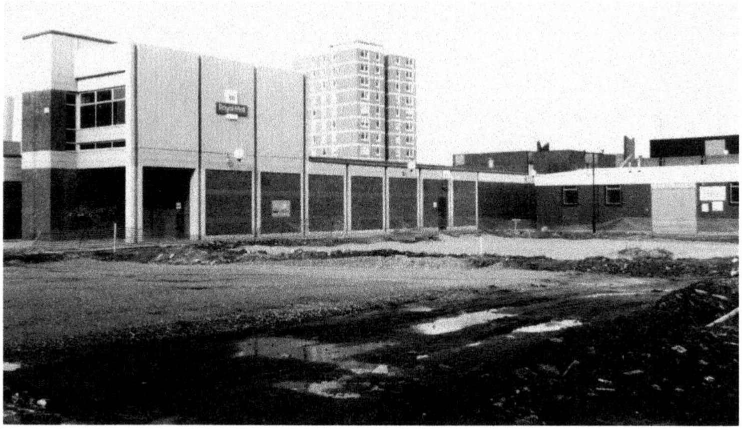

General Post Office

The relocation of the General Post Office from North Street to Monkton Road during the 1960s was a welcome addition to the modern facilities that were now available within the town centre. However, the council's decision to enforce traffic-calming measures by re-routing traffic from Monkton Road created much disruption. Shopkeepers from the Arndale Centre complained continually to the borough council, without success, in a bid to overturn their decision and replace the bus route along Monkton Road, which was having a devastating effect on lucrative passing trade. The area was eventually developed into a car parking and pedestrianised zone. Pictured: ground resurfacing and creation of car parking facilities at Monkton Road in 1973.

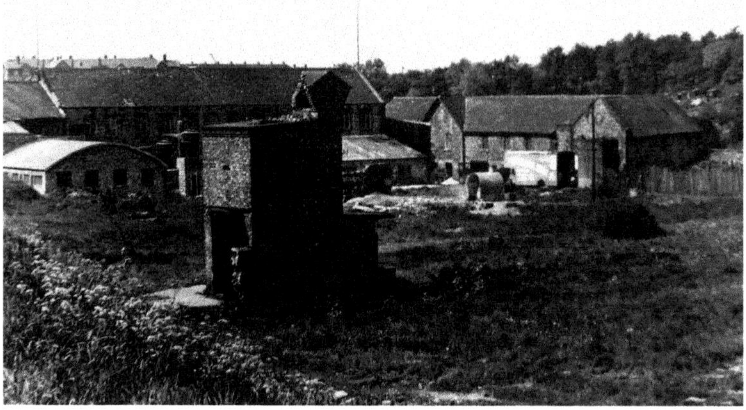

Springwell Paper Mill

The site of the former paper mill at Springwell Road lay derelict for several years until it became a vital asset to Jarrow Corporation when it was utilised as the Jarrow Instruction Centre during the 1930s. By the 1960s and 1970s, the old mill was used initially as a warehouse by Smith's Furnishing Company. This was followed by several firms that were attracted to the warehousing facilities. The final resident to vacate the premises was Kenton Utilities, which was when the area was reclaimed for further development. This image dates from 1960.

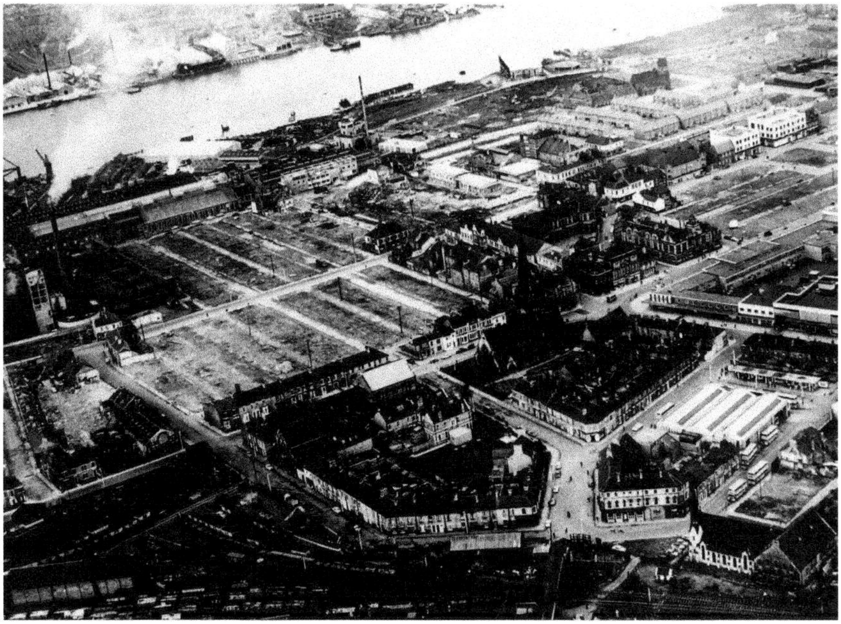

Central Area

The disappearance of much of the central area becomes evident when one studies the accompanying aerial photograph from 1964. The white buildings (upper right) were occupied by the now defunct Jarrow & Hebburn Co-operative Society until they relocated to Centenary House in the Arndale Centre around 1970. From this time, the building was converted into bar and restaurant facilities, otherwise known as the Cavalier Club.

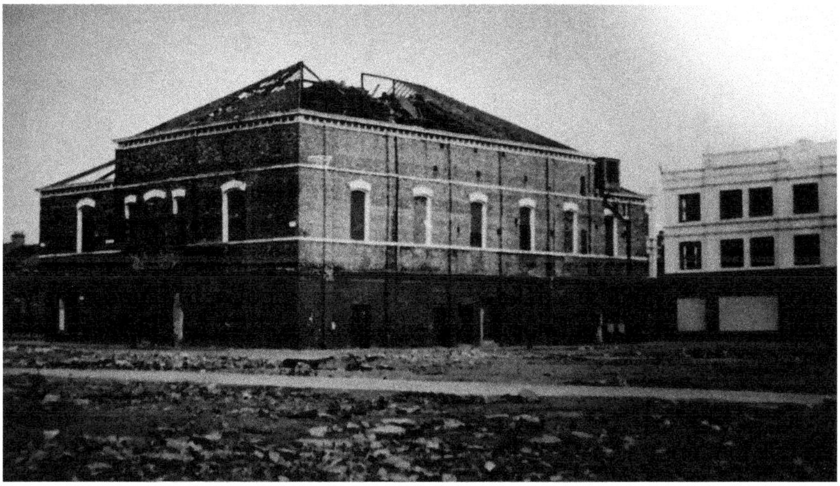

Market Square

The Market Square development site became available in 1963 after the successful demolition of the old Theatre Royal, the spoils of which created the Lindisfarne Roundabout at Primrose.

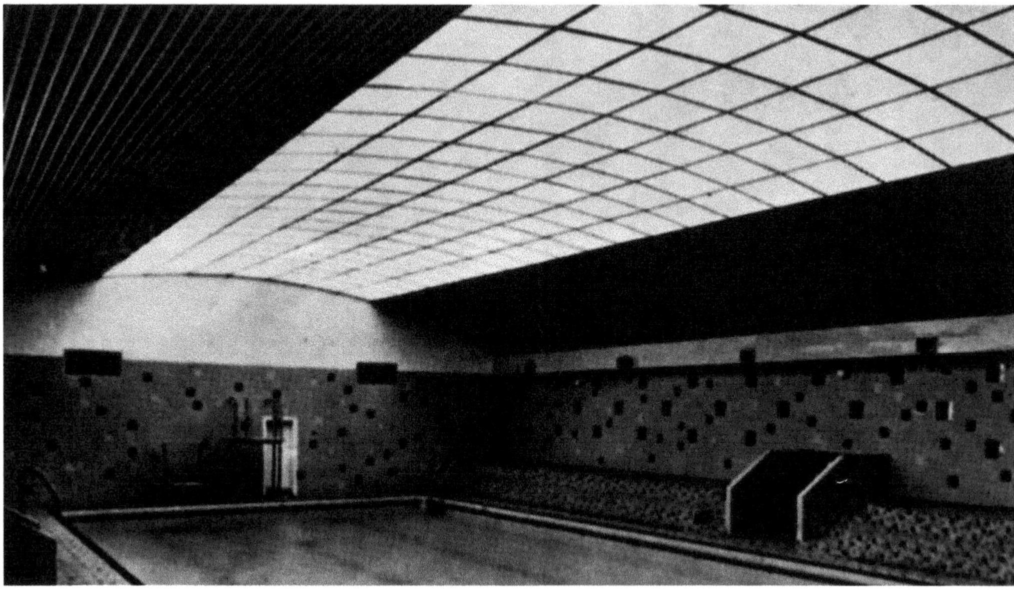

Slipper and Swimming Baths

The slipper and swimming baths, pictured in Walter Street in 1966.

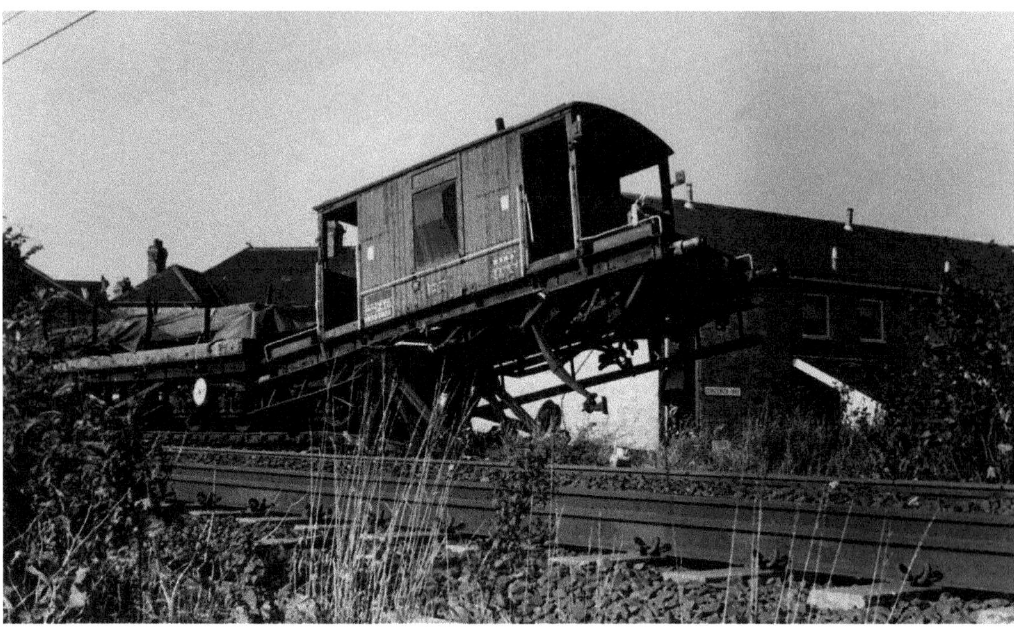

Derailment at Jarrow

A guard's van from a cargo train hangs precariously in the balance close to housing in Concorde Way, where it careered through railway barriers in October 1984 on the mineral line close to Jarrow railway station. It was feared the disabled train would leave the rails careering down the embankment into the property below. Emergency services and railway personnel reacted accordingly, preventing any further damage.

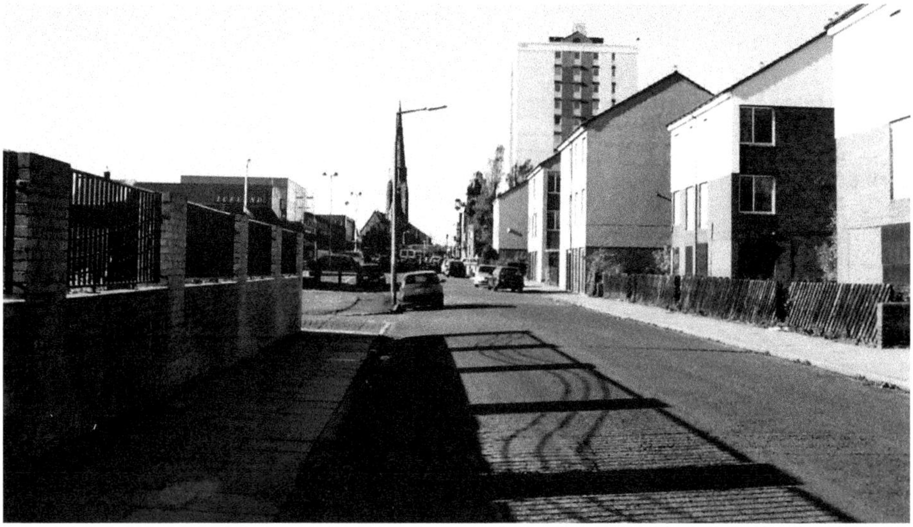

Grange Road

Precious little of the original Grange Road exists today, with the exception of the Town Hall and Christ Church, visible in this image from 1980. One of the town's three cinemas, the Regal was located in this formerly busy thoroughfare. Built in 1866, the cinema then was known as the Kino. Prior to this time, the site was occupied by Foster & Hornsby's cabinet works, and later, prior to the Walter Street facility from 1911, slipper baths and wash houses.

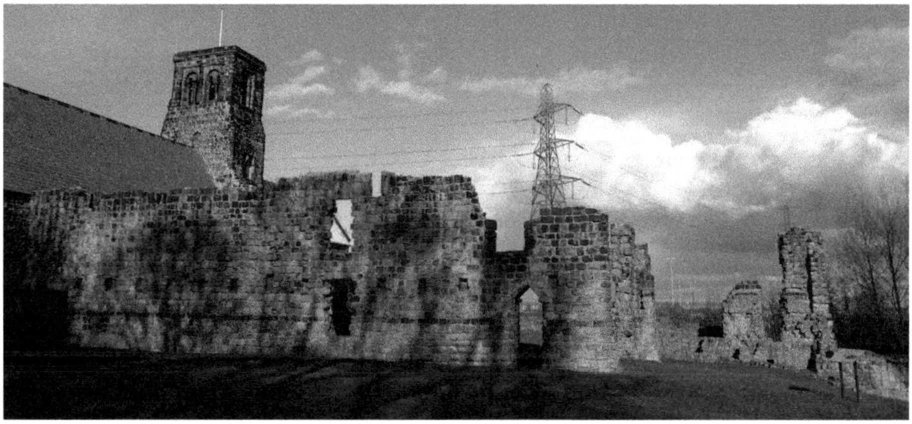

Population Boom

The population of Jarrow has risen dramatically ever since the Gyrwe tribe resided in what we know today as East Jarrow, around the sixth century. At this time a census was barely necessary to record the few heads that populated the area. Centuries later, it was the Palmer empire that was responsible for the influx of Irish immigrant workers to Jarrow during the 1920s. It was this influx that swelled the population to an excess of 40,000 people. Since the 1970s, the population in recent times has maintained a steady but sustained reduction, fluctuating between 27,000 and 33,000. Pictured: Seventh-century monastery ruins.

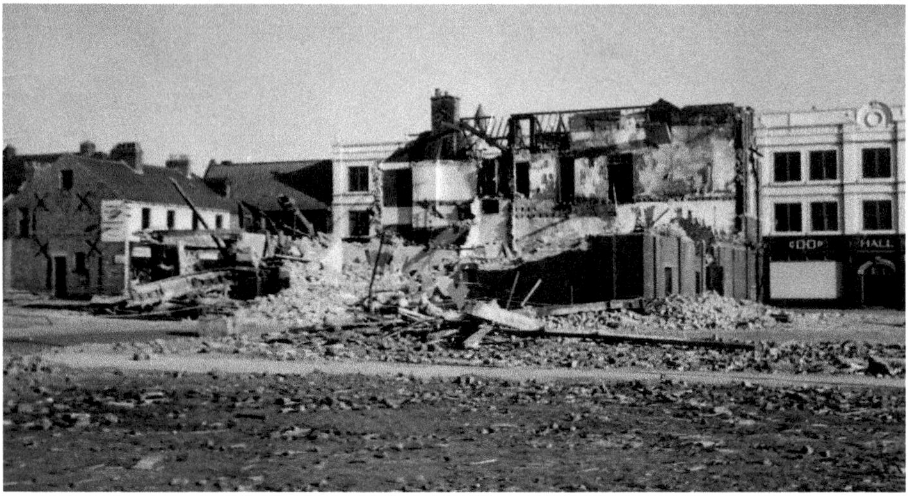

Theatre Royal

Another wonderful and evocative image from 1963, showing the partial demolition of the Theatre Royal and Market Square.

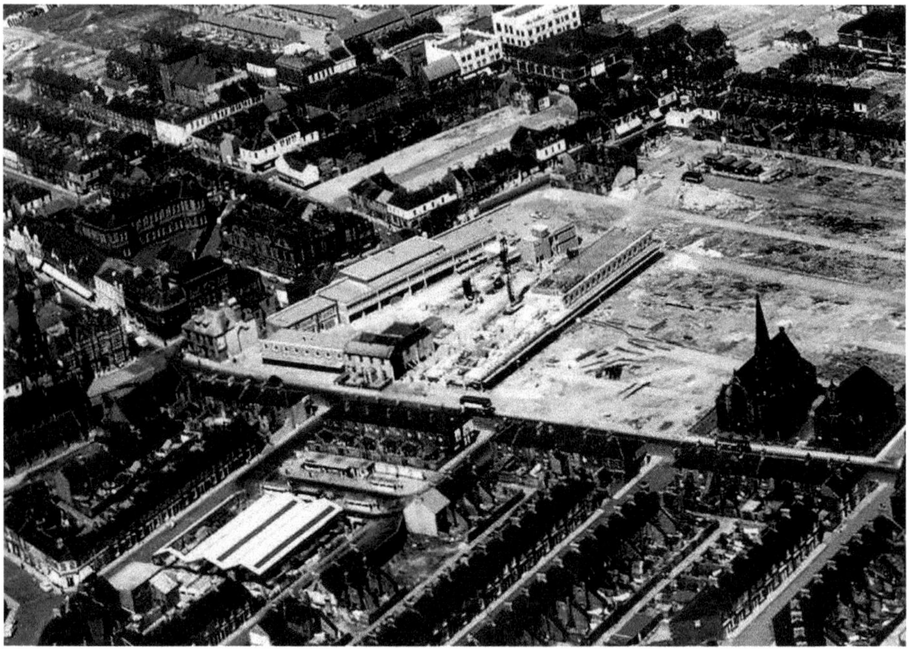

Central Jarrow

This 1960 image of the central area was taken just prior to the inauguration ceremony of the completion of phase one of the Arndale Centre in 1961. It is worthy of note how much of the town was still intact around this time. However, this image would have told a different story if it had been taken just three years later, as best part of the town centre had been demolished. Pictured: A 1960 aerial view of the town centre.

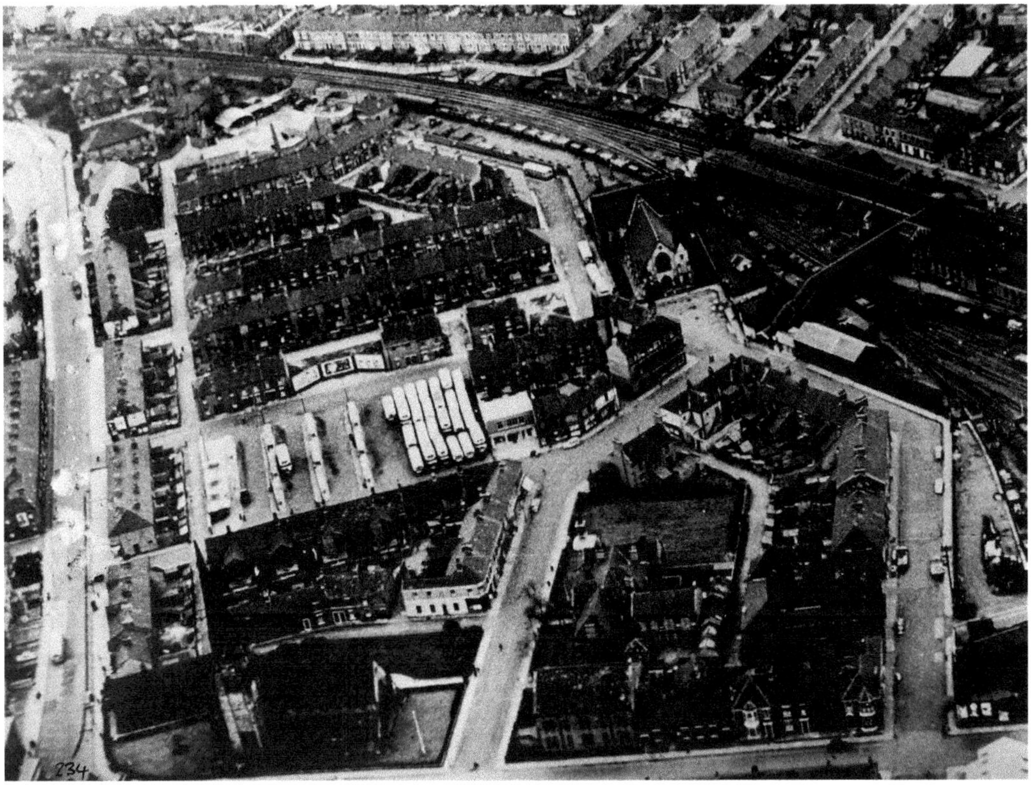

Central Jarrow

An interesting aerial photograph of the heart of the town from 1960. The only buildings to survive the redevelopment of the town centre is Christ Church, Baptist Church and a terrace of houses in Grange Road West. Practically everything else was demolished this side of the railway station, shortly after this photograph was taken. The former LNER railway lines, coal depot and station stairs are clearly visible on the upper half of the photograph.

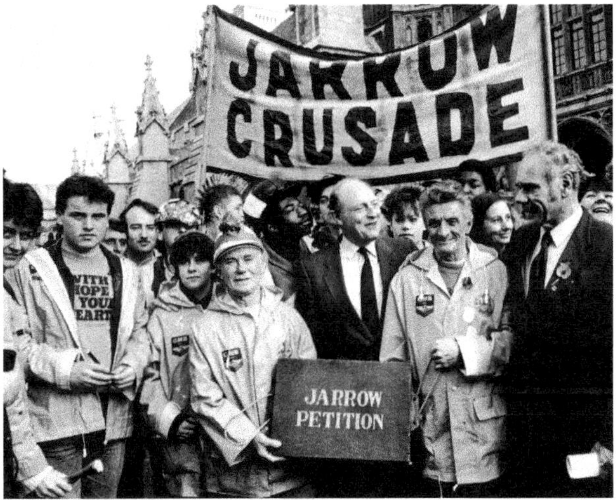

Jarrow Crusade Demonstration

Member of Parliament and former Labour leader Neil Kinnock, pictured here with Jarrow MP Don Dixon at Trafalgar Square, London, in 1986. Speaking on behalf of a delegation from Jarrow, who were protesting the unemployment situation, on the fiftieth anniversary of the Jarrow Crusade.

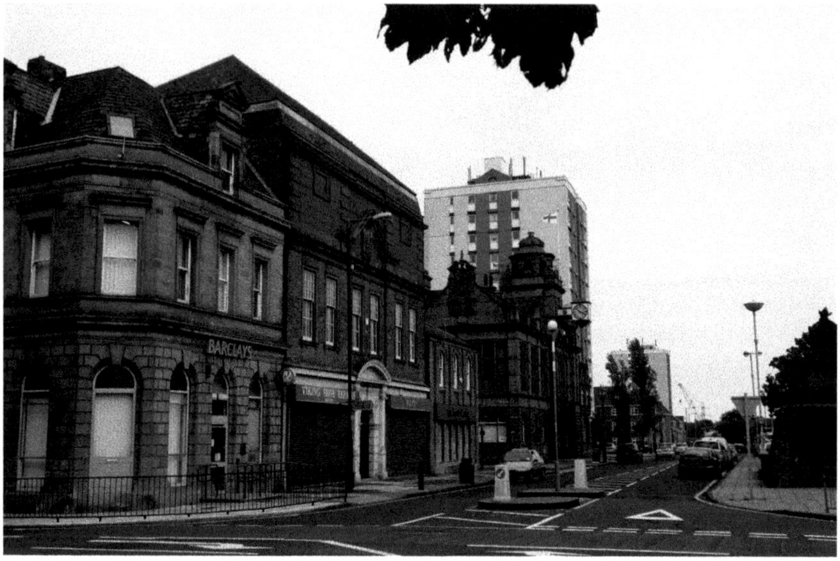

Town Centre

Radical changes to Jarrow town centre became inevitable as the construction of modern-style housing got underway in Grange Road during the 1960s. The only buildings to survive the demolition were those illustrated in this photograph from 1988, Sunderland & South Shields Water Authority, the Masonic Hall and the Town Hall among them.

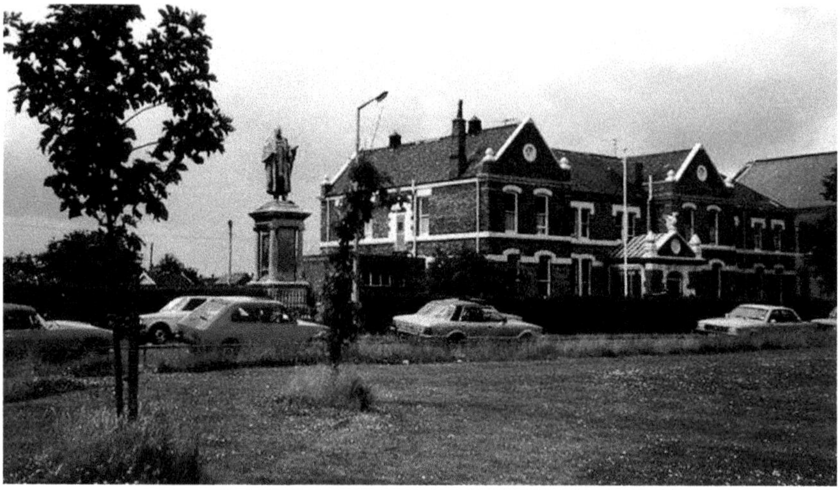

Palmer Memorial Statue

Formerly positioned within the grounds of the Palmer hospital in 1904, Albert Toft's statue, dedicated to the great industrialist Sir Charles Mark Palmer, was relocated to a site overlooking his beloved River Tyne during the 1970s, in preparation for the construction of a more modern hospital. After bouts of vandalism to the bronze statue, a decision was made to relocate the monument in 2007 to a site opposite the Town Hall in Grange Road.

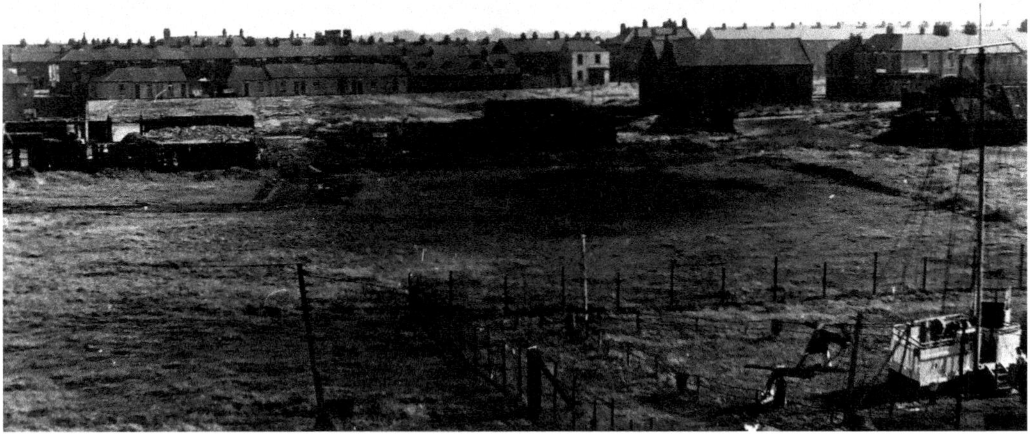

Sea Cadet Corps

Jarrow's association with the Sea Cadet Corps commenced in 1939. The headquarters were situated on the site of the former cricket pavilion in Curlew Road. Because of its isolated location, the premises were subjected to successive acts of vandalism, until the building was eventually declared unviable and irreparable. By 1962, sufficient funds had been raised to erect a prefabricated structure on the existing site, and two years later in 1964, the Jarrow division took residency of their new headquarters under the command of Lt Cdr Barrington RNR.

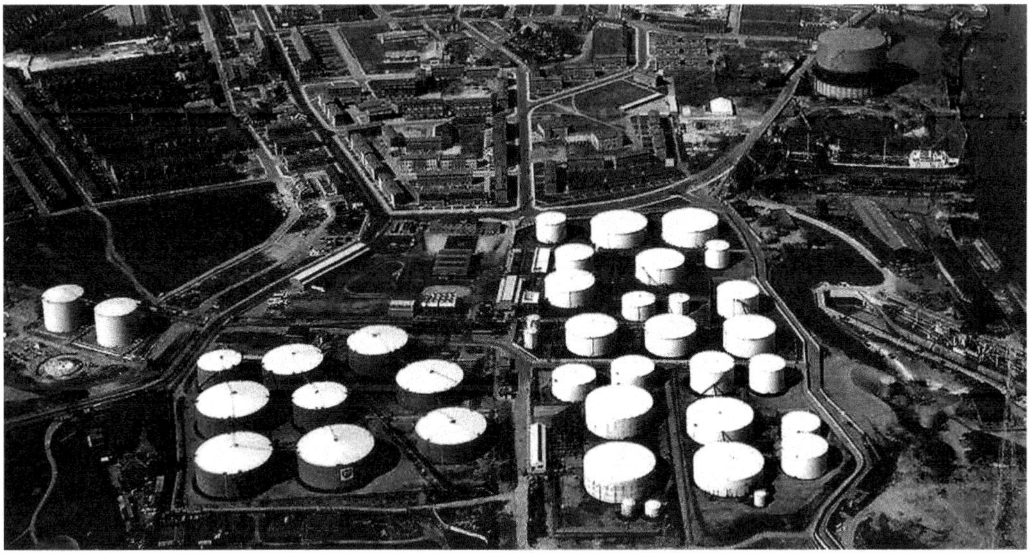

Oil Storage Facility

Barren land at this part of Jarrow was largely given over to industry. Isolated from the main body of the town, the area was utilised by Shell Mex & British Petroleum Ltd for the safe storage of combustible liquids in the form of petroleum spirit and fuel oils. During the Second World War, this area became the unsuccessful target for enemy bombing raids in 1941. This photograph of the plant dates from 1970.

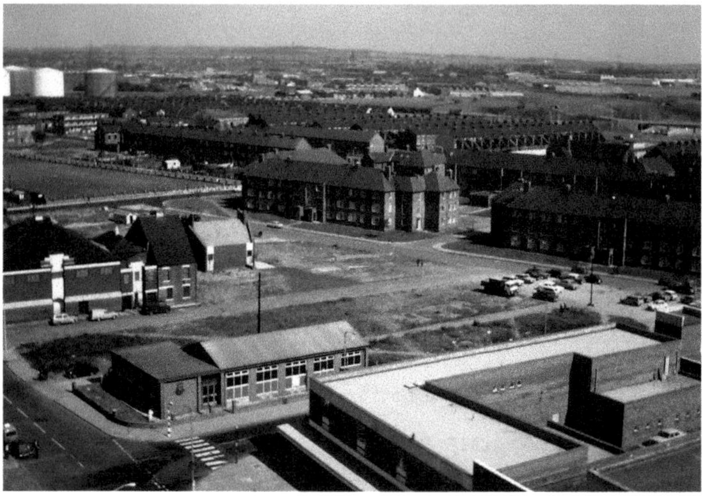

Bird's-eye View of Town Centre

Not quite an aerial shot, but nevertheless a perfect vantage point to record and demonstrate just how dramatically the townscape has changed in the past fifty years or so. This image is from 1967, when the festival flats were still habitable and in reasonable condition. To the left of the image are the old Regal cinema and the Salvation Army citadel.

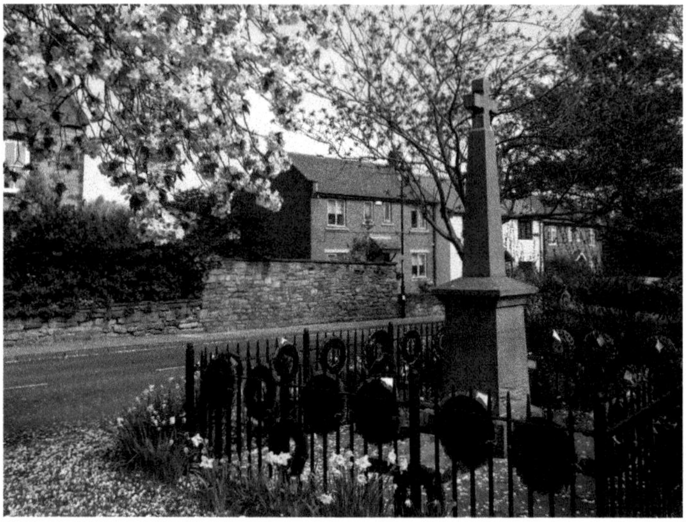

Monkton Village

This was the idyllic scene of the ancient village of Monkton and the Church of the Venerable Bede. The war memorial to the right of the photograph was erected in 1921 as a lasting tribute and respect to those who fell in the First World War. As the decades passed, the savage northern elements stripped the monument bare of the names of those to whom it is dedicated. Members of the Royal British Legion refurbished the sandstone memorial to its former condition during the 1980s. The scene is further enhanced annually with a carpet of springtime daffodils and a cherry blossom.

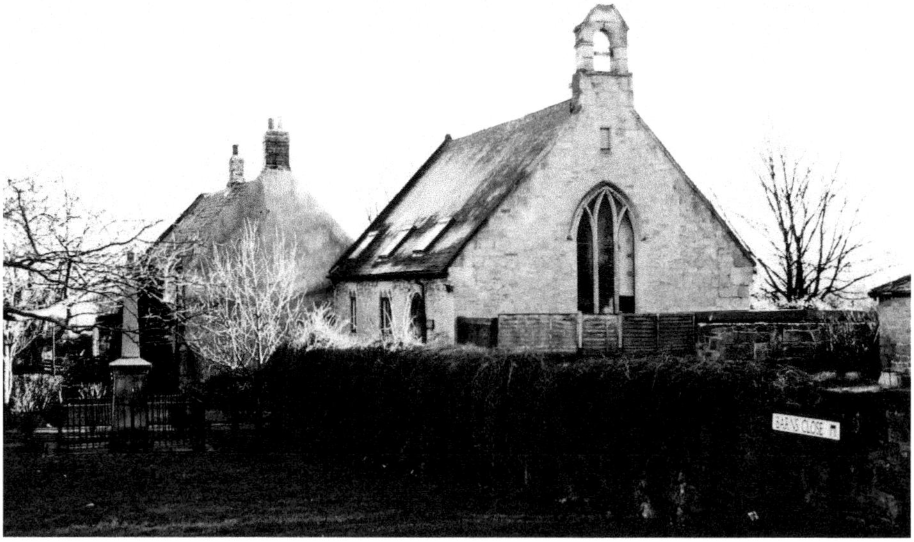

Venerable Bede Chapel of Ease

The ancient Venerable Bede Chapel maintained its status as a place of worship up until the 1960s. Sadly, during the 1970s, the building was abandoned, falling into a state of disrepair. But the voice of conservation was heard, and the listed building was eventually saved from destruction, refurbished and converted into a fine residence.

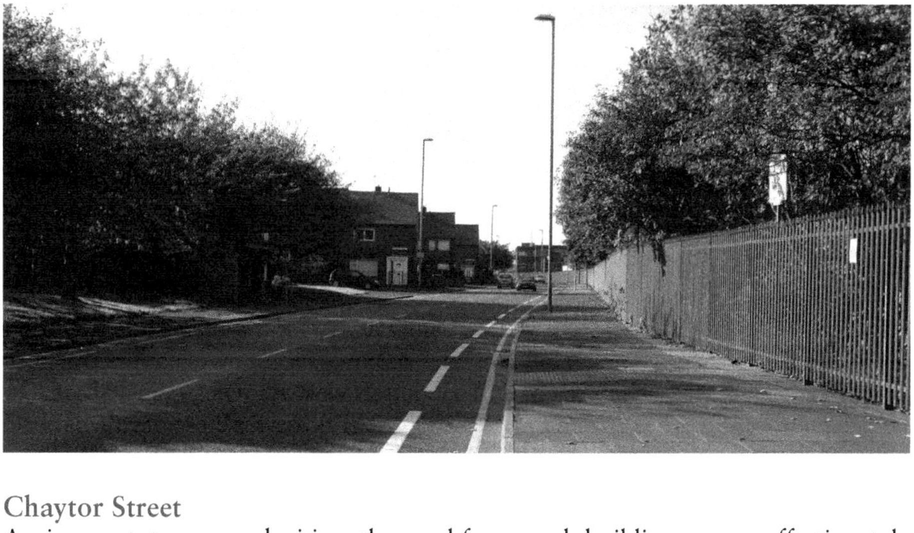

Chaytor Street

As in most towns and cities, thoroughfares and buildings were affectionately named in honour of local dignitaries, business people and Aldermen of the relevant boroughs and the towns they represented. Chaytor Street, which has formed a ring road around the town since the 1960s (pictured here in 1989) was named in honour of Alfred Henry Chaytor, a New Zealander who inherited Jarrow Hall from his uncle Drewett Ormonde Drewett. It is from this man we get the names Ormonde Street and Drewett Playing Fields – or Charlie's Park, as the latter is commonly known.

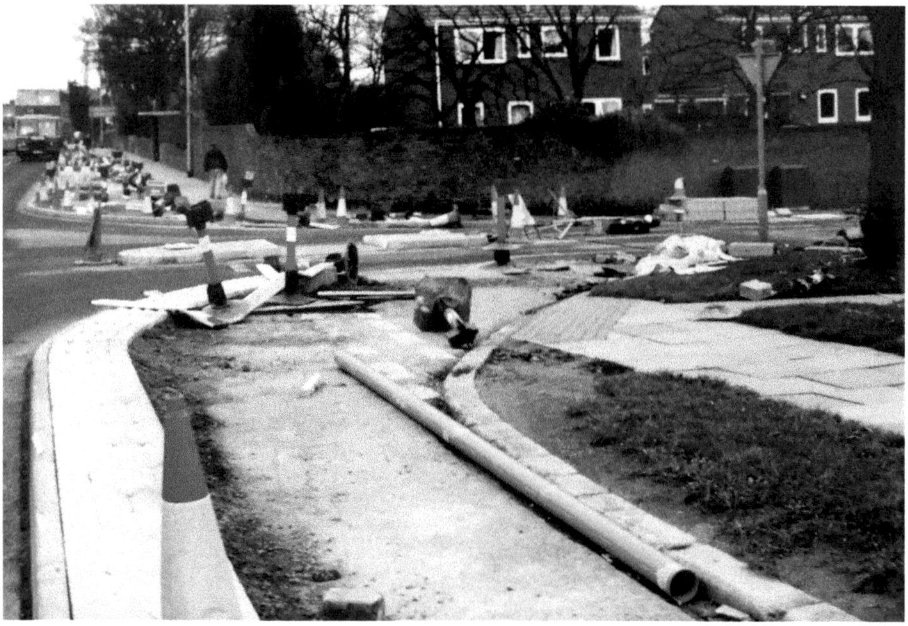

York Avenue

Above and below: The intricate network of road markings, mini roundabouts and traffic bollards most of us have to encounter on a daily basis is evidence of the volume of traffic on today's highways and byways. The carving up and narrowing of traffic lanes and the introduction of a cycle lane on one of the town's most picturesque thoroughfares, York Avenue, has only been in operation since 1989. Prior to these traffic-calming measures, it was a one of the country's first dual carriageways, dating from 1928.

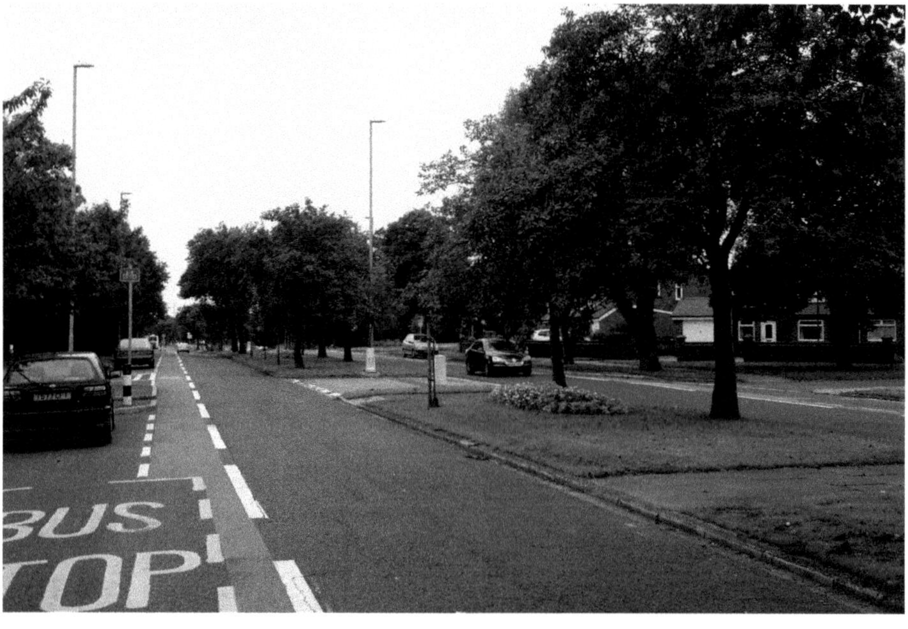

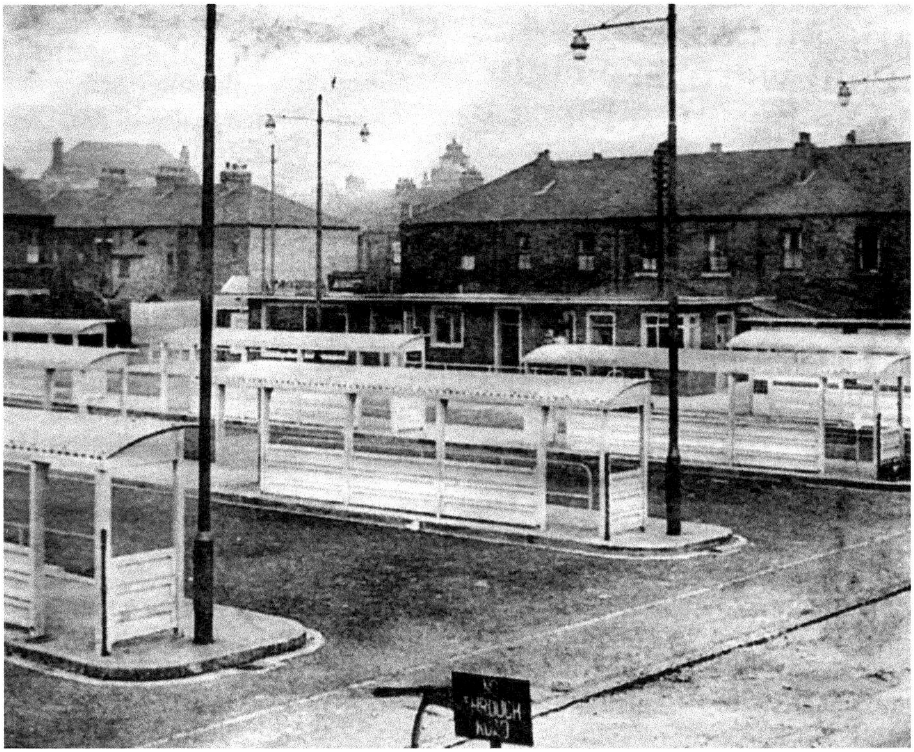

Bus Station

Above, below and overleaf pages: After the Second World War, people were becoming more familiar and dependent upon public transport. Northern General Transport (NGT) operated fleets of buses from South Shields, Newcastle and Durham, offering destinations to most parts of the North East. South Shields had an electrically operated trolleybus service powered by overhead cables. This was a very swift and pollution free economical service, but it was limited to inner towns and cities. Eventually, the trolleybuses were discontinued in favour of the more modern and versatile motor bus,

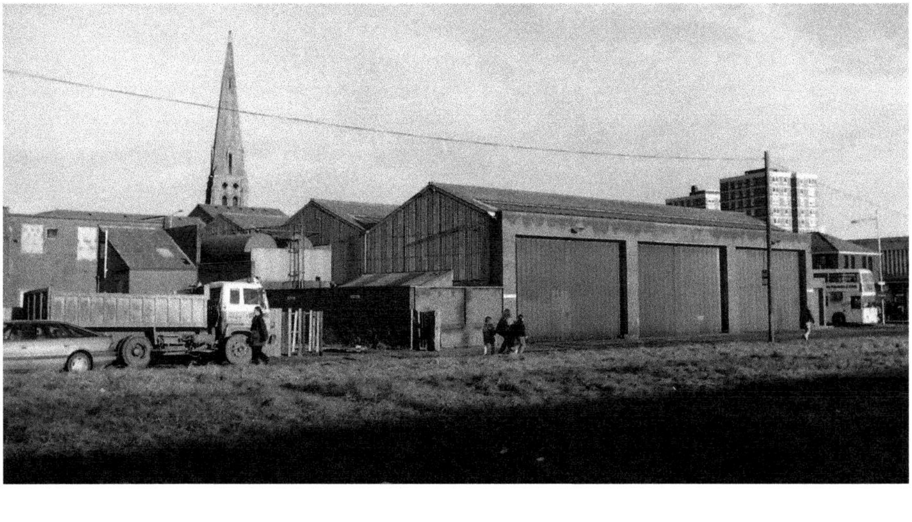

which were garaged locally at Mile End Road, South Shields. The need for more depots became evident as NGT's fleet multiplied. The Jarrow depot came along in 1954 to a convenient site in the town centre. By 1988, a depot of this size was deemed uneconomical, as more passengers were now using the metro system as their chosen mode of transport. After the former bus station was demolished, a scaled-down version was erected close to the original site, serving the town equally as well as its predecessor.

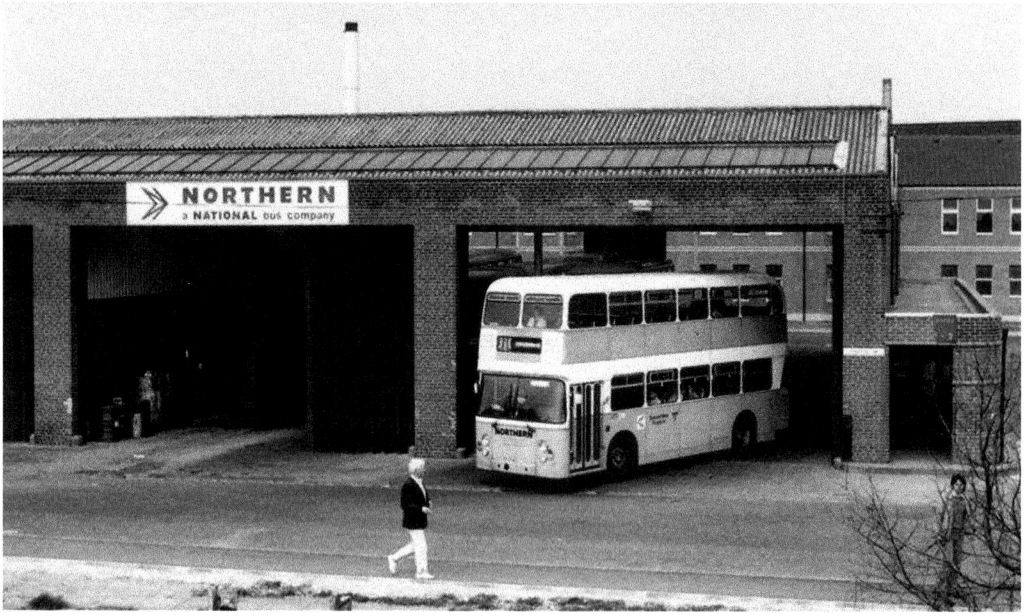

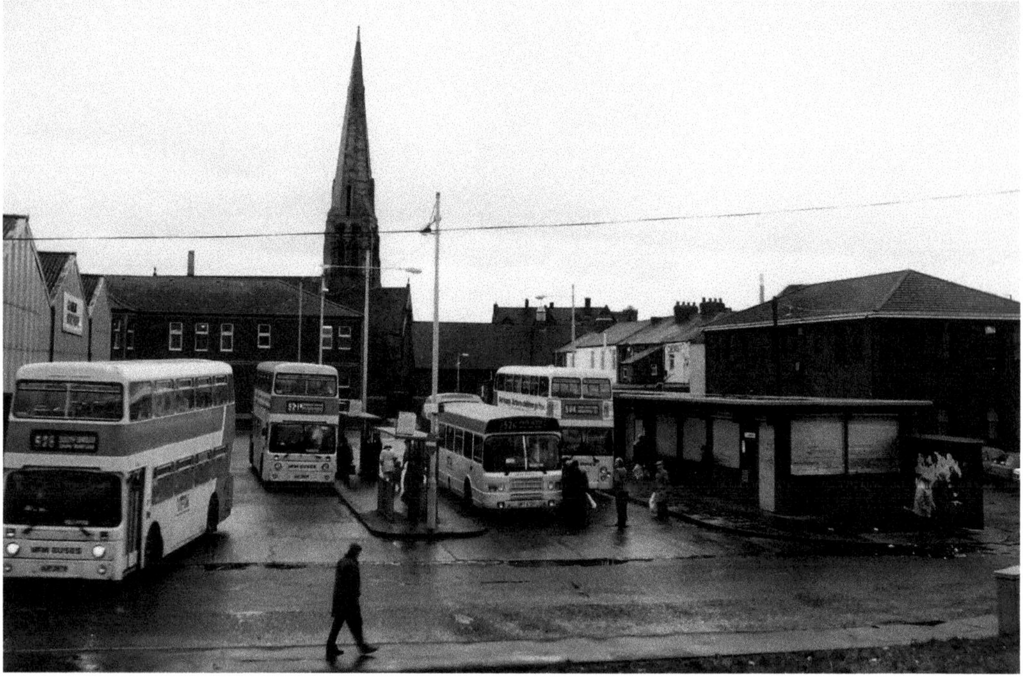

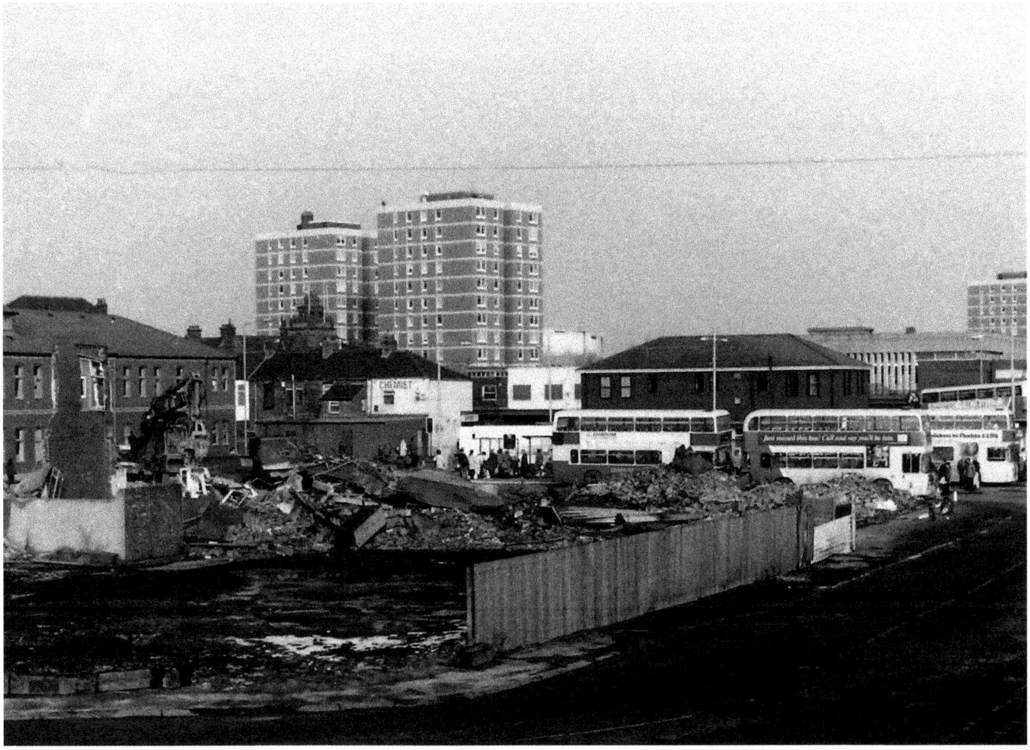

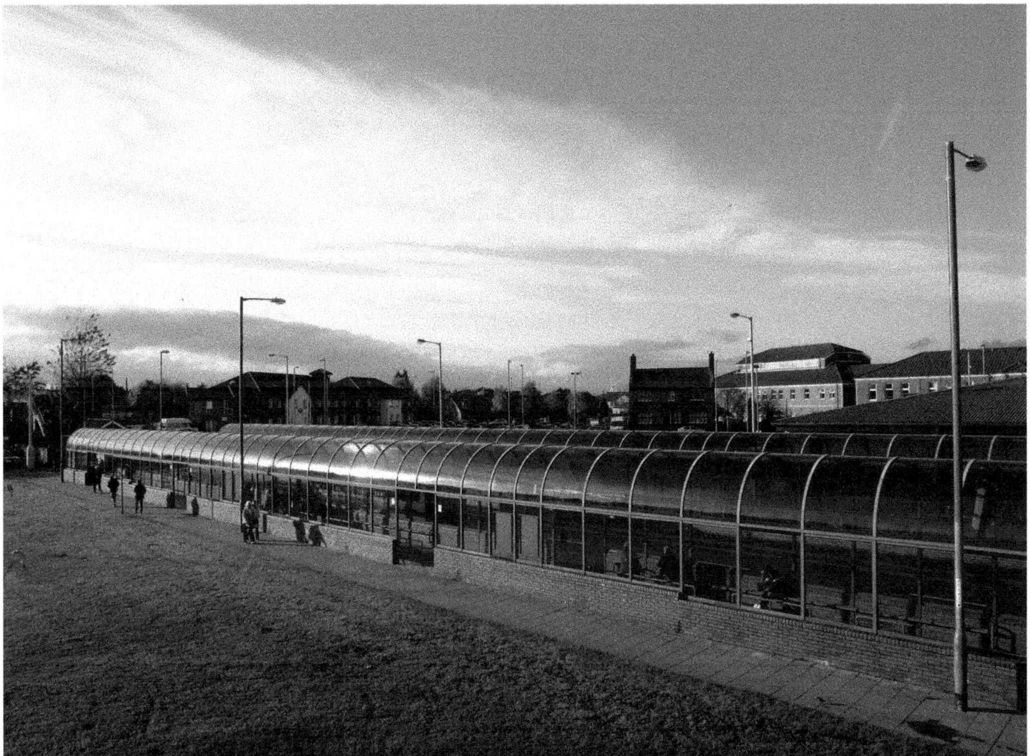

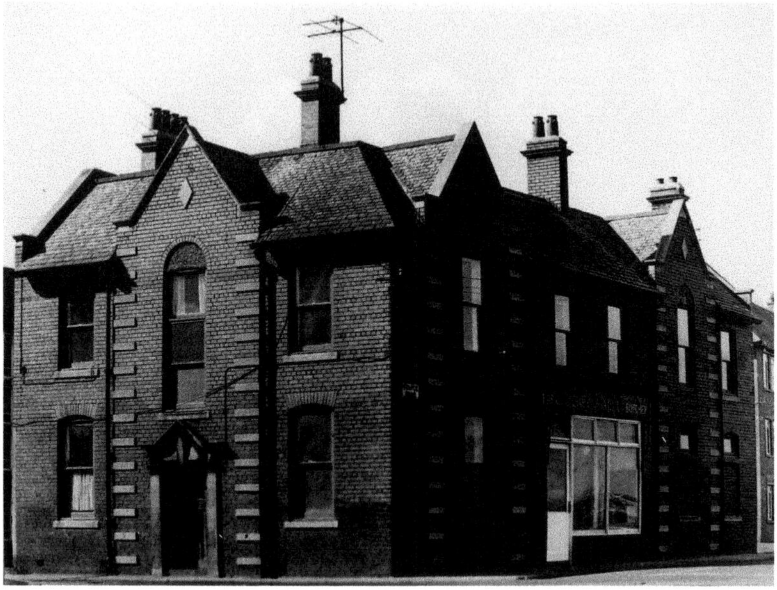

High Street

This former residence situated in High Street was constructed in 1912 for German pork butcher Henry J. Abel, who resided in the property, as did his family, until the late 1960s. Since this time, the property has changed ownership on several occasions and has been substantial enough to support a variety of business ventures.

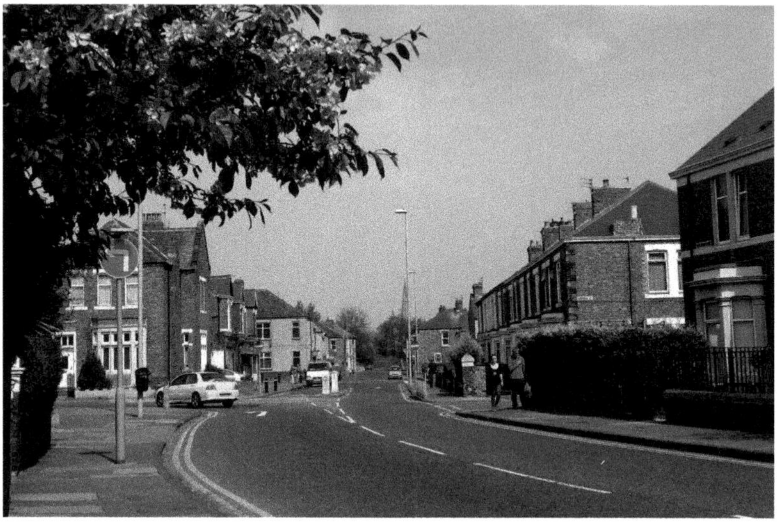

One-way System

In 1970, and much to the displeasure of residents, the council decided to implement traffic-calming measures at the junction of Bede Burn Road and Surrey Street. The one-way system eased congestion considerably at this troubled spot. So successful was the scheme, which was originally put in place as an experiment and temporary measure, that it still survives today.

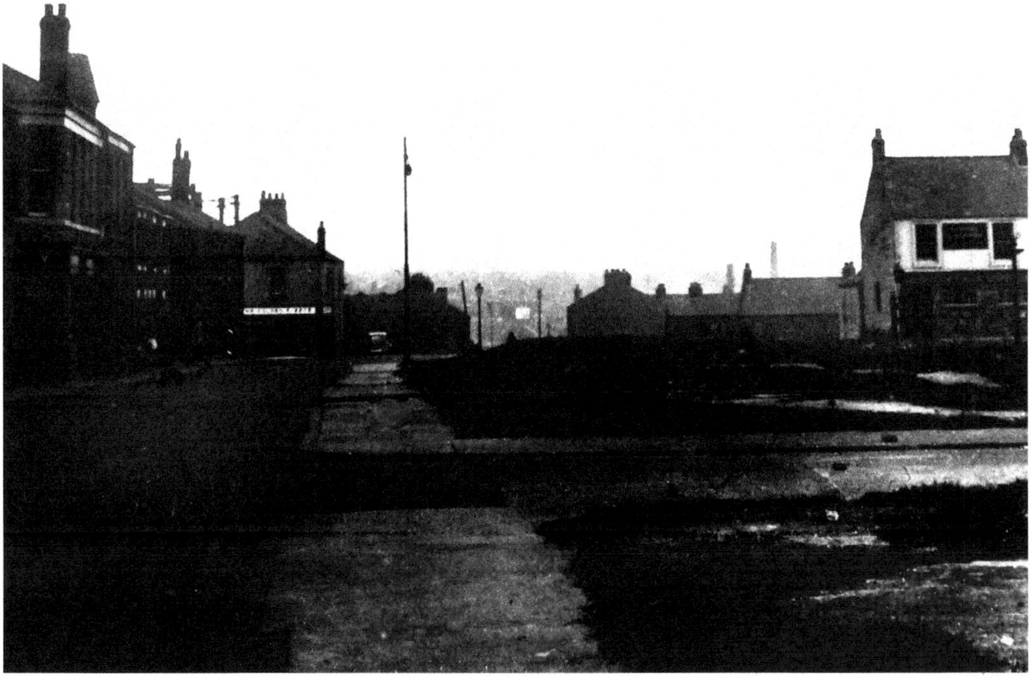

Ferry Street

Apart from the river crossings at Gateshead and other significant Tyne crossings designed for both traffic and foot passengers, others were accessible in Jarrow, Hebburn and South Shields via a ferry service. The foot-passenger service at Jarrow was discontinued in 1952, when the pedestrian tunnel became available, but was retained solely for vehicular traffic until 1967 when the service became obsolete at the inauguration of the road tunnel. Ferry Street, visible in the accompanying photograph, was the principal thoroughfare, providing access to both pedestrian tunnel and ferry services.

ACKNOWLEDGEMENTS

Dedicated to the people of Jarrow, for countless years of loyalty and encouragement. You're too numerous to mention individually, but too important not to mention at all.

I am most grateful to the following organisations and individuals who assisted during my research for this publication:

Newcastle Chronicle & Journal
Newcastle City Libraries
South Tyneside Reference Library
Shields Gazette
David Morton
Malcolm Perry
Michael Joyce
Joe Anthony
Lorrain Hillas
Angela Snowden
Lawrence Cuthbert
John Joyce
Anthony Paul Perry
Jimmy Flaherty
Fengzhi Zhang Bayles-Rea